DETOUR

a side trip through chemotherapy and poetry

November 2013 to September 2014

Diana Vidutis

eLectio Publishing

Little Elm, TX

Detour: A Side Trip Through Chemotherapy and Poetry
By Diana Vidutis

Copyright 2017 by Diana Vidutis. All rights reserved.
Cover Design by eLectio Publishing.

ISBN-13: 978-1-63213-336-6
Published by eLectio Publishing, LLC
Little Elm, Texas
http://www.eLectioPublishing.com

Printed in the United States of America

5 4 3 2 1 eLP 21 20 19 18 17

The eLectio Publishing creative team is comprised of: Kaitlyn Campbell, Emily Certain, Lori Draft, Court Dudek, Jim Eccles, Sheldon James, and Christine LePorte.

Publisher's Note
The publisher does not have any control over and does not assume any responsibility for author or third-party websites or their content.

To Nida

My Spirit

And Mantas

My Soul

Gratitude

I would like to thank first and foremost the team at the Sidney Kimmel Cancer Center at Sibley Memorial Hospital in Washington, DC, for the fact that I am still here today ~ my oncologist, Dr. Katherine Thornton, my nurse Natasha Shultz, my gynecological surgeon, Dr. Jeffrey Lin, and my gynecologist, Dr. Anandi Kotak. Thank you also to my acupuncturist, Eve Soldinger, and to my friend Dr. Rafael Convit who convinced me to go to her to supplement my chemotherapy with adjunct medical healing.

Thank you also to my family and friends who showered me with attention and affirmations and prayers and love during this crisis. It was much like attending your own wake.

My brother Neil (and his wife Sally) from Cincinnati spent a week here while I was in the hospital recovering from surgery. My brother Linas came in from Ann Arbor to be with me for a couple of rounds of chemo. My sister Aldona and my mother sent constant support from Cincinnati.

Mostly, thank you to my friends who stepped up to take me to and from chemo, to spend the night when necessary, to bring food and flowers and good wishes, and to keep me feeling normal ~ the Divas Isabelle and Jura, the Vaiciulaitis sisters Danute, Joana and Aldona, Micaela, Ernie and Rafael, Angele, Jurate, Vilija, Dale and Algis. Thanks to my bootcamp instructor Vameka for making me strong. Thanks to the members of Trinity parish in Georgetown who, at another Jurate's request, prayed for me for many months, neighbors Nancy and her daughter Ana Palomino, Barbara, Richard and Sherri, Mary, and Arnetta, to name a few. And to the extended family that is the Lithuanian-American Community, who lent me purpose and moral support.

I am very grateful to the law firm of Winston and Strawn for the excellent medical coverage, for making it possible for me to continue working throughout chemo, and to my wonderful co-workers, whose company and encouragement bolstered my health in so many ways.

Thank goodness for the everyday purveyors of poetry such as Garrison Keillor and his "Writer's Almanac" (which I hear on public radio every morning at 6:45 am, then get by email that same day), Karen and Mike Garofalo and their GardenDigest, The Poetry Foundation, and www.goodreads.com. You will see that, after describing the mechanics of chemotherapy, I turn to poetry to try to find meaning in it all. And poetry did not disappoint. Poems start making their appearance about halfway into this story, soundly taking over by the end.

Thank you to Ellen Cassedy who always encouraged my writing, and to Indre Martinson for suggesting that I turn the emails into a book. And to the friends to whom I sent my updates of "Diana at Chemo" that became the "Detour," who responded to my daily emails with validation, appreciation for the poems, and valuable insights of their own.

Finally, and most importantly, I am forever grateful to my children, Nida and Mantas, who, although adults in their early twenties and successfully "launched," made me feel like I was still essential to their lives.

Hymn to God, My God, in My Sickness
BY JOHN DONNE (1572–1631)[1]

Since I am coming to that holy room,
    Where, with thy choir of saints for evermore,
I shall be made thy music; as I come
        I tune the instrument here at the door,
        And what I must do then, think here before.

"I am so sorry for your diagnosis"

It happened over vacation. Labor Day weekend. Bethany Beach, Delaware. For the third year in a row, I had rented a small house for a week with a friend of mine. My kids were in their twenties and I was 10 years into menopause when I started having a period again.

My friend was a single mother now, too. We'd been coworkers who'd lost our jobs together in 1988, become pregnant after that, had sons born a few days apart, gotten new jobs, gotten our divorces over the years, and lived not far from each other. Bethany Beach was a 3-hour drive from our homes in Maryland.

She had summered at Bethany with her family as a child. I had enjoyed a few days there with my kids when they were very little, and fell in love with the kind of house that was modern but had a screened-in porch running the full length of the inside. When I found one to rent for a week, I was ecstatic, and came back to the same house the next year and the year after that.

So here I was, early September 2013, enjoying the sand and the sea, the restaurants and the shops, and the general slow-paced family atmosphere of Bethany Beach. Our adult children were free to come and go. This year, it was her son and his bride who stayed for a few days.

Out of the blue, little by little, I had cramps and then noticed I was bleeding, like a teenager. Over vacation. Suddenly, I found myself cruising the feminine hygiene aisle of the beach pharmacy. It was astounding how flat sanitary pads had gotten over the past decade. It was shocking that I should be shopping for them at all after so many years.

But there was a logical explanation for this physical development. A year and a half before, just after turning 60, I had decided that I wanted to get more physically fit. I figured I had a good thirty if not forty years still ahead of me. I wanted to make sure the blood would continue to flow through my veins unobstructed, that no plaque would be allowed to develop, and I wanted to get rid of my lower back pain. Yoga was not enough.

I chanced upon a Groupon for a boot camp in my neighborhood that met at 5:30 am, and it seemed a perfect solution. Instead of lying in bed listening to NPR news weekday mornings, I would get out and exercise. We had a gym at my K Street office, but I wasn't organized enough to gather shampoo and outfits the night before. Plus, I didn't want to sweat in front of my colleagues. A 5:30 am session gave me enough time to shower and dress at home and be at my desk by 9 am. It was ideal.

Over the next 18 months, literally by sweating each ounce off, I dropped two dress sizes (from a 12/14 to an 8/10), gained great strength in my core (as evidenced by my being able to genuflect easily 28 times on one occasion), and, as my 22-year old daughter remarked, "You've got a waistline, Mom!"

Obviously, or so I thought, I had fooled my body into thinking it was younger than its years, and it had decided it was time for me to reproduce again. But, just like the middle-aged mother in Thomas Mann's "Black Swan," who falls in love with her son's young tutor and is heartened to start menstruating again, this was not a sign of youthful vigor. It was an indication of uterine cancer.

There is no history of cancer in my family, other than prostate that many men seem to get as they age. I am a firm believer that we all have cancer cells lying dormant in our bodies. When and why they get activated remains a mystery.

Mine was a bolt from the blue. A lightning strike on a beautiful day. A Deus Ex Machina phenomenon.

It was my good fortune that it presented so dramatically. You can't ignore bleeding for very long. And mine didn't go away after two weeks, as my regular internist expected (who, by the way, said it was unnecessary to conduct pelvic exams on women such as myself more frequently than once every 5 years). I went to a gynecologist at that point.

A Pap smear would not have uncovered my cancer, they say, but we'll never know. On the other hand, early detection doesn't always lead to better outcomes. Often, it just leads to knowing you have cancer for a longer period of time. Who needs that.

In my case, less than the two weeks before my second appointment with my gynecologist, I was bleeding so much I thought I might exsanguinate. Having never used my health insurance for a non-routine visit, I was pleasantly surprised to get a human being on the line who actually approved me to call my provider. There was a 24-hour nurse who listened to my symptoms, consulted with an on-call doctor, and recommended that I get myself to the George Washington University emergency room. I will be forever grateful to my daughter's friend who drove me there on a Friday night, to my daughter who met me there by metro (after I'd convinced her to go out because I was fine), to the emergency room staff who took such good care of me.

Like most women, I hate pelvic exams (as, apparently, did my internist!) but here I was getting more of them than I'd ever counted on. Included was one of those vaginal ultrasounds that the Virginia legislature wants to punish women requesting an abortion with. It wasn't awful, but by then, I was in resigned patient mode.

Thank goodness, the gynecologist with whom I had an appointment the next Monday scheduled me for a dilation and curettage (D&C) that very Thursday. The other option had been an outpatient biopsy, which would have had me jumping off the table. She needed more tissue, and I was fine with being knocked out.

"Yes, you have cancer, and it's serious." I had taken a friend with me to the follow-up appointment where I would get the results, and I was glad I did. She asked questions as I sat there in shock. I got a little weepy but not really upset. I had already come to the conclusion that I could deal with the diagnosis if it turned out to be cancer. I could face a hysterectomy. That I could do.

And I did, with the help of my brothers who flew in to be with me, my mother and sister who gave support from afar, and great friends at my side. I also had a very supportive employer who kept paying my salary in full over the eight weeks it took me to recover from the surgery and to get started on the chemotherapy.

I was much more afraid of the chemotherapy than of the operation itself. I'd had a Caesarean section with my son, so I knew what to expect. Difficulty coughing, blowing your nose, laughing. It's amazing how much you use your stomach muscles.

Since they needed to remove the uterus intact, this was not laparoscopic surgery. I now have a surgical cross on my stomach, horizontal from the C-section 25 years ago, and vertical from the hysterectomy.

The hospital gave me a heart-shaped pillow to hold against my wound when I needed to cough or sneeze. That helped. But I was the second patient in a two-person room, and my half accommodated a bathroom and the passageway to the other patient's half, so it was more like ¼ of a room, with no window.

But when you're recovering, you are just happy for the visitors and the flowers and the good wishes. Bodily functions take priority. Walking. Walking. Walking.

When I learned from my oncologist that they did, indeed, plan to give me chemotherapy, I thought, "I can do that." I'll just stop by over lunch once every three weeks, get a dose for an hour or so, and then go back to work.

But when they told me that, no, it would not be one hour every three weeks but nineteen hours, over several days, every three weeks, I thought they were trying to kill me! I went to get three other opinions, including from the guru of my disease at Sloan Kettering, but they all recommended the same procedure and basically the same chemicals.

So I concurred.

I would do the chemotherapy I thought I didn't need. "Just to make sure to get any cancer cells that may have traveled throughout your system." They had cut out my uterus, my ovaries, my fallopian tubes, and 19 lymph nodes. Who knew that your lymph nodes continue draining for weeks after an operation? I felt so sorry for women who'd had breast cancer. They have to wear special tubes to collect the fluids that continue to drain from the lymph nodes in their underarm areas. Mine, from my groin area, just drained out the usual way. I felt very lucky.

I had no idea how lucky. Lucky to have a tumor that could be removed, along with surrounding tissue, and still leave me able to eat and drink, walk and talk normally, without pain. I could breathe. I could digest and eliminate. I could eventually resume my life.

"I am so sorry for your diagnosis," said my gynecologist when she read it to me. "I am so sorry for your diagnosis," said the gynecological surgeon, in our pre-operation consult. "I am so sorry for your diagnosis," said the pathologist, the mother of my daughter's friend, after viewing my report. She assured my daughter I would live to see her graduate from law school, as if that were a comfort. When she heard about the chemotherapy regimen planned for me, her reaction was "They're going for a cure!

I could accept cancer, but I could never quite accept that it would terminate my life, at least not right away. It is always better to have a manageable tumor to remove than a metastasized one that needs to be shrunk with chemotherapy so that surgery can follow. Chemotherapy weakens your immune system, thereby making surgery difficult. On so many levels, I was most fortunate.

And I have a new lease on life, however tenuous.

On the Beach at Night Alone
Walt Whitman, 1819 - 1892[ii]

On the beach at night alone,
As the old mother sways her to and fro, singing her husky song,
As I watch the bright stars shining, I think a thought of the clef
    of the universes, and of the future.
A vast similitude interlocks all,
All spheres, grown, ungrown, small, large, suns, moons, planets
All distances of place however wide,
All distances of time, all inanimate forms,
All souls, all living bodies, though they be ever so different, or in
    different worlds,
All gaseous, watery, vegetable, mineral processes, the fishes, the
    brutes,
All nations, colors, barbarisms, civilizations, languages,
All identities that have existed, or may exist, on this globe, or
    any globe,
All lives and deaths, all of the past, present, future,
This vast similitude spans them, and always has spann'd,
And shall forever span them and compactly hold and enclose
    them.

Subject: Diana at Chemo ~ Day One! 1.
8am Tues Nov 19, 2014

This is for anybody who wants to get updates from me as I go on this journey through chemo, hopefully to a cure!

Please let me know if you want to keep getting these.

I find the whole experience kind of fascinating myself.

It helps to have excellent doctors, nurses, and medical insurance.

So here goes!

I am here at Sibley Hospital in Washington, DC, in the first hour of chemotherapy. The ultimate chemical combination will be ifosfamide and paclitaxel to combat something called an MMMT (malignant mixed mesodermal tumor, or "mixed Mullerian" for short). Another name for my disease is carcinoma sarcoma. Plus, there's a little rhabdo-myosarcoma thrown in, usually found only in children.

In any event, I had all my baby-making equipment removed about 6 weeks ago, and now I have to make sure none of the bad stuff pops up elsewhere. It had already jumped to one lymph node; hence, the need for chemotherapy.

So far this morning, I have been infused with one liter of saline. No searching for veins in the arm though. About 10 days ago, I had a port implanted below my right collarbone. It is amazing how well the body heals. Now, there is just one prick to access that bump below the skin where that catheter was installed, and all further infusions and blood draws will be unnoticeable.

Next comes about another hour of infused pre-meds: a steroid Decadron and Zofran against nausea, Zantac and Benadryl to counter any allergic reactions, and an "Emend" pill for nausea.

After that, the poisons, er.... medicine mentioned earlier will be administered. That's when any side effects should kick in.

I will keep you posted.

Right now, I am sitting in a very comfortable recliner in a large, open, window-filled floor outfitted with cubbied booths that can accommodate two people at a time. Have my own TV, bookshelves, plus there's Wi-Fi. We can eat whatever we brought with us whenever we want. I am looking forward to a big dinner at home tonight.

I have also been given a "Patient Guide" binder describing the treatment plan, with tabs for "managing side effects," "coping," "surviving cancer," and information on where to buy wigs.

My oncologist, and her stand-in, have already been by. People are discussing Thanksgiving plans. I have booked a flight to Detroit for Thanksgiving 9 days from today. My immediate goal is to meet my 6-month old grandnephew!

Just yesterday and the day before, I was running around Manhattan, meeting up with old friends, slipping in a consult at Sloan Kettering. The temperature outside was 60 degrees.

My son met me en route from Helsinki to San Francisco. We took in the Rockettes Radio City Music Hall Chrwitmas spectucular. Tried to live life normally.

I may be fading out now from the Benardyl. Then the poison/medicine will be administered shortly.

Over and out. 10:15 am.

Diana at Chemo ~ Day Two! 2
4:30 pm Wed Nov 20, 2013

Once again, this is for anybody who wants to get updates from me as I go on this journey through chemo, hopefully to a cure!

Please reply to me if you want to keep getting these.

You will know if I've gotten your reply if your name appears in the "to" section.

I must be in honeymoon chemo.
Today's session lasted only 5 hours.
Then my friend picked me up and we went out for Thai food
Last night, friends came over for dinner.

I don't feel any side effects yet, except for a slight metallic taste in my mouth that disappears with blackberries or grapes. They pre-medicate seriously for nausea (Zofran) and give me Mesna pills to protect from renal attacks by the Ifosfamide.

Today's chemo started with $1^{1/2}$ hours of hydration, a half hour of Zofran, and the remainder Ifosfamide.

I don't feel any needle because the catheter inserted into my port yesterday was capped off for re-use the next two days.

I almost think I should have chosen the option to get chemo at 21st & K Streets because I feel well enough to work, and I could get there by metro.

Then again, I'm supposed to be avoiding germs...and pets...and gardening.

Renee lounged next to me at chemo yesterday. She drives herself in, sleeps with two cats and a dog in her bed at home, has a great wig, and laughs at the notion of buying mascara when you forget you don't have eyelashes anymore.

I'll wait for my daughter to arrive this weekend to dig in the remaining tulip bulbs for me. My son left this morning but he did kitty litter duty, which I'm no longer allowed to.

Yesterday was a long day at chemo, but the Benadryl knocked me out for 4 hours, so it really was like taking a long overseas flight. The place was almost empty when I left at 5 pm, but I noticed an athletic-looking young man, probably a high-schooler, being infused, with his Dad accompanying him. That's a heartbreaker.

So today was a pleasant surprise. One more day, then in on Friday for the $5000 Neulasta shot to beef up my white blood cells.

So glad I have good health insurance.

Subject: Re: Diana at Chemo ~ Day Three! 3
4:30 pm Thur Nov 21, 2013

When I got home from chemo yesterday, there was a message from the doctor at Sloan Kettering wanting to discuss the pathology report from Sibley. That sounded a little ominous, but I heard from her later today. She just hadn't gotten all the requested unstained slides from them, only slides of the lymph node, with the rhabdo tumor, and nothing from the uterus. So the two doctors will talk directly and straighten it out. Sloan wants to do its own pathology. It wasn't done when I visited Sloan on Monday.

Today was another breezy day at Chemo. I basically slept through most of the 5 hours. A friend from the neighborhood drove me over and picked me up. I am so glad to be able to go home in the evenings. The original plan to do a more aggressive treatment, focusing on the rhabdo and hospitalizing me for three days, was very discouraging. I hope they don't go back to that.

I feel puffy and like I'm retaining water, but the nurse claims that's very normal, and it will all drain away in a few days.

I no longer have a needle capped in my port. No more access until 2 weeks from now! Not that it hurt at all, but it made bathing awkward....

Tomorrow, I go in for an injection to increase the white blood cells, which are due to plummet. Then I have a session with the acupuncturist who will assess my reaction to the chemo.

My doctor wants to me to get a CT scan on Monday to see if, "heaven forbid," something might have developed since surgery 6 weeks ago. It entails drinking barium, lots of it, for two hours in advance. All for the good.

Have to get some face-masks for the flight on Thanksgiving Day to Detroit. Wish I had a hijab.

Subject: Diana at Chemo ~ 4
8:30 pm Fri Nov 22, 2013

Once again, this is for anybody who wants to get updates from me as I go on this journey through chemo, hopefully to a cure!

My day was fine, but I was quite shaken at the end to learn that a neighbor, who organizes our annual Christmas caroling in Takoma Park, has been suffering tremendously for the past six months with colon and pancreatic cancer.

In comparison, a shot to build up my white blood cells, followed by acupuncture, sounds positively spa-like.

They keep saying I will lose my perkiness. Ten days after the start of chemo is when it's supposed to first hit. That would be right at Thanksgiving. My family will understand.

My acupuncturist told me my body was "depleted," although I don't feel that. She's had a lot of experience with cancer patients. Says everything is cumulative.

So far, so good, and I'm very grateful for that.

Subject: Diana at Chemo ~ 5
6:15 pm Sat Nov 23, 2013

My daughter is now home and will show me shortly how to put the emails into proper blog form.

Off to the movies this evening to see "Gravity" with her. I guess I should wear a face-mask.

Warded off the metallic taste all day with snap peas and green grapes.

I think the Vietnamese noodle soup Pho is good for me.

Greatest accomplishment today was purchasing a wig in the neighborhood! Walked into a very unprepossessing place on Georgia Avenue. My daughter and I looked at one that appeared promising. I tried it on, and we are happy! Great style – I'll have to ask my regular hair to be cut this way. Made in Japan. Lovely salesperson, also named Diana, at Crown Wigs who recommended against real hair wigs (that cost thousands of dollars) ....

Subject: Diana at Chemo ~ 6
11:00 pm Sun Nov 24, 2013

Once again, this is for anybody who wants to get updates from me as I go on this journey through chemo, hopefully to a cure!

I understand that my ability to be out and about, go to a movie, go to church, have dinner with friends, be able to drive — these are all things to be very grateful for.

My first week of chemo, which seemed so frightening, starting with a 7-hour day, and then two 5-hour days, I survived well.

Today's Mass was in memory of a young mother who died this month of breast cancer, leaving her husband and a 7-year old son. I am so thankful my children are grown. I got to enjoy motherhood. It would be nice to be a grandmother, too, someday, but it almost seems like a luxury.

On the other hand, I meet people everywhere who are cancer survivors. I'm part of a club now. They are all around us.

CT scan tomorrow. I will try to pretend the barium is egg nog...

Subject: Diana at Chemo ~ 7
6:45 pm Mon, Nov 25, 2013

Yesterday, Georgetown's streets and red brick sidewalks were brightly carpeted in yellow ginkgo leaves.

Today, we scrambled to rake up the carpet of red maple leaves in our front yard ahead of the approaching leaf vacuums.

When is a chore a delight? When you realize you may not get to do it again....

It took me 38 gulps to drink down the first quart of barium today.
Two hours later, it took 44 to get the second quart down.
Some iodine in the arm that feels warm in the body and metallic in the mouth once released, a ride on a gurney

through the donut hole a couple of times, and the CT scan is over.

I indulged in a Big Mac and fries afterwards, feeling incredibly guilty, knowing I should be drinking kale shakes. But the point is to move matters along. Greasy food always works.

I hope to go back to work the first week of December, for one week.

Then chemo for one week. Then two weeks of work. If they will let me.

Subject: Re: Diana at Chemo ~ 8
10:30 pm Tue, Nov 26, 2013

Felt like I was having chest pains today, and realized that's probably the Neulasta kicking in from Friday's injection. The nurse had said it would affect the large, marrow producing bones first, like the sternum and the pelvis (who knew?). Just noticeable, not really painful.

So no sooner did I reveal my slip down into McDonald's for comfort food yesterday than the millennials got all in a tizzy and are taking charge of my diet. I already know about drinking green tea and putting ginger, garlic and turmeric into everything, but the kale shakes I will let them create. Scallions and leeks are major warriors, as are any cabbages. I love Brussels sprouts, broccoli, and cauliflower, plus all fruits, and eat plenty of them. Did you know that rice is bad for you? Because of the arsenic used in its harvest?

So we had quinoa with organic chicken from Whole Foods tonight. Paid $7.49/pound (!!!!) for the flattest chicken breasts I have ever bought. Usually, I can slice the chicken breasts I get for $2.49/lb in half sideways. Ah..... is it that their plumpness derives from synthetic growth hormone? And I have foisted these upon my children their entire lives?....

My daughter has taken to heart the nutrition guide from the "Anticancer" book by David Servan-Schreiber. It's just common sense, but it does tweak nutrition for its highest cancer-fighting properties. The best diets are Mediterranean, Indian, and Asian. And never eat grapefruit while you are on chemo.

I indulged in some red wine with dinner and, I must say, I feel the best I've felt since chemo started. Plenty of green tea on the side, but I am feeing almost normal.

Subject: Re: Diana at Chemo ~ 9
11:00 pm Wed, Nov 27, 2013

Kale shakes are not so bad. In fact, the ones my daughter made for me were so good that I had to sneak seconds. They can look green and disgusting but, once you put in strawberries and bananas and orange, you don't taste the leek or the kale or the turmeric at all. It's just light and refreshing.

Speaking of leeks, when I wrote yesterday "Scallions and leeks are major warriors" I meant "warriors" in inhibiting cancer growth. Others are garlic, Brussels sprouts, broccoli, cauliflower, all cabbages, spinach, onions and, of course, kale. It's good that I like all of those vegetables, and perhaps I'll get to like kale.

My doctor left a message that my scan on Monday was "good" but that she wanted to speak some more with me. I hope she's not hoping to go for the more aggressive treatment.

She says she left a message with my workplace that I could start again on Monday. That would give me six days of work before the next chemo.

I wonder if Southwest Airlines will let me board early tomorrow if I say I need to avoid germs because my immune system is compromised by chemo. Hopefully, no one will want to sit next to a lady in a face-mask, so my daughter can get the seat next to me...

Happy Thanksgiving! Off to Detroit in the morning!

Subject: Diana at Chemo ~ 10
Thurs Nov 28, 2013
Thanksgiving Day, Detroit

It worked!

I can attest that every airline passenger will avoid at all costs sitting next to a woman wearing a surgical mask on her face.

Southwest allowed me to board early.

I had read that it is safest to sit closest to the bulkhead in order to avoid germs.
So I took a middle seat in row two, and absolutely everyone passed me by until the plane was practically full.

I told the brave woman who finally asked if the aisle seat next to me was taken not to worry, that I was not contagious.

She was relieved.

And I thereby managed to save the window seat for my daughter who boarded almost last.

It was a pleasant surprise to land in a wintry Michigan landscape.

I was so happy to meet 6-month-old Wesley, the first great grandchild in the family.

And to be able to indulge in all the traditional food and drink of Thanksgiving.

By the way, Airborne does work. I was fighting off sniffles before boarding this morning and have no more symptoms.

It was also reassuring to talk with my nephew's mother-in-law who had gone through chemotherapy 30 years ago and was going through it again now. She says the strides that have been made in managing nausea and easing infusion are phenomenal. By using ports, there are no more burning veins and multiple punctures to cope with. And the anti-nauseals administered preclude the need to have a bucket at your side. It gives everyone hope.

There is nothing like a baby to brighten up a gathering of adult family members.

But I was most impressed by the night-vision baby monitor.... available as an app on your iPhone.

Subject: Re: Diana at Chemo ~ 11
10:00 pm Fri, Nov 29, 2013

I feel like someone who has been told to take antibiotics for 10 days, then feels so much better after 3 days that temptation sets in not to bother taking them anymore.

No fatigue. No hair loss. I feel totally normal and healthy. Perhaps we don't need to go on with that chemo.

Just wishful thinking....

Visited the Matthaei Botanical Gardens of the University of Michigan today. At the entrance to the tropical house is a memorial bench dedicated to my beloved late sister-in-law, Britt Andersen Bieliauskas, who was an avid gardener and great lover of natural beauty. She died at age 50 of multiple aneurysms. We miss her greatly.

The surrounding ponds of the gardens are almost frozen now, but it was sunny and pleasant enough this afternoon to stroll the trails. We ended up at a paved labyrinth that I walked. The one here was in the "Baltic" style, used in Scandinavia and Germany.

Since then, I have come across labyrinths in many other places, including cathedral floors. I remember the move to install a labyrinth outside Blair High School in Silver Spring, Maryland. Interestingly, over the six months it took the organizer, her husband, and volunteers in the community to build the labyrinth — made of more than 1,100 stone pavers on the lawn outside Blair — the project became more personal. It became a place where she found strength as her own husband fought cancer.

As with acupuncture and meditation, I am a skeptic but I try. Walking a labyrinth is a practice that has been around for 4000 years, and is shared by many religions and cultures. Walking close repetitive loops that circle to a center is supposed to have intrinsic value as a "self-alignment tool" intended to clear the mind and give insight. I walked it in the middle of a prairie in winter. Do I wonder why.

Subject: Re: Diana at Chemo ~ 12
11:00 pm Sat, Nov 30, 2013

Still in Ann Arbor, closing down Thanksgiving weekend with food, family, the Michigan-Ohio football game, a flat tire, a little shopping, and a few movies.

Just living normally, spending precious time with the young adults (aged 21 to 37) who are the next generation of our family.

From my 90-year-old mother to my 6-month-old grand nephew, how important it is to "just be" ("tik būk" in Lithuanian).

Subject: Diana at Chemo ~ 13
10:30 pm Sun Dec 1, 2013

Going back to work tomorrow for the first time since my surgery October 9th!
Second round of chemo will start Dec 10th.

In the meantime, some tidbits I've picked up along the way...this from David Servan Schreiber's "Anti-Cancer A New Way of Life"

"The Mantra and the Rosary"

Practices that bring forth the harmonization of biological rhythms for well-being and health go back to the most distant past.

There is even a suggestion that the rosary was introduced in Europe by crusaders who received it from the Arabs, who had in turn adapted it from practices of Tibetan monks and yoga masters in India.

"In Italy the congregation recites the rosary taking turns with the priest. Each recitation occurs in a single exhalation. The inhalation that follows takes place during the priest's turn. The subjects had quite naturally adopted this rhythm while reciting the prayer during the experiment. In doing so, they had adjusted which happens to the natural rhythm of fluctuations in the other biological functions (heart rate, blood pressure, blood flow to the brain)."

So... the recitation of Hail Mary 50 times, Our Father 5 times, and Glory Be 5 times may serve a purpose similar to that of a mantra ...

Subject: Re: Diana at Chemo ~ 14
11:00 pm Mon, Dec 2, 2013

The ketchup at the airport had an odd, weak taste.
The spaghetti sauce at home was not very good, either.
It seems that tomato is one of those foods affected by chemo.
The doctor told me that that's not unusual.
Also, my scalp is beginning to tingle.
This part I am not looking forward to.
Another tidbit I have learned, and that I am not particularly
fond of.

From O. Carl Simonton's "The Healing Journey"

The tendency to attribute the cause of cancer to the person
suffering it, or "psychological characteristics of people
before they were diagnosed with cancer"

- responding to stress with a sense of hopelessness
- bottling up emotions or having impaired emotional outlets
- perceiving a lack of closeness with one or both parents

Personality characteristics are said to be tied to survival
rates. Plus there are "disease-prone personalities."

It all seems a bit harsh.

Subject: Diana at Chemo ~ 15
10:00 PM Tue, Dec 3, 2013

I wonder about the day when I wake up and leave my hair on the pillow.

They say it happens that way.

Just not to me quite yet.

My first two days back at work have been wonderful.

There were quite a few looks of shock in the office, as if I had returned from the dead.

And quizzical glances, since I look about the same as I did two months ago.

There's a lot to be said for uneventful and normal.

Now let us honor all menstruating women.

There is nothing like being in menopause for 10 years and then being thrust back into full-blown menstruation to make you realize how tough it all was.

That is how my uterine cancer manifested itself. I was free of menstruation for a decade, and suddenly it all came back again.

But it also gave me a renewed appreciation for all of the pain, discomfort, and embarrassment that women go through so gallantly for 40 years of their lives.

Yes, it is compelling to have a bodily function tied the to the phases of the moon, but all that cramping and bleeding for so many years was really miserable.

We should be giving up our seats on the metro to all women of childbearing age.

Subject: Diana at Chemo ~ 16
11:15 pm Wed, Dec 4, 2013

Made my own kale smoothie this morning for breakfast, and it was delicious!
My daughter has started a Pinterest page called "Anti-cancer recipes."
I also read about detoxifying using oil in one's mouth.

And my hair is coming out now, right on schedule, in loose handfuls...
I've made a small soft nest on the table next to me.
I hope I still have enough on my head for the office Christmas party on Friday, but I might have to pull out the shag wig.

Spoke with a former colleague, much younger than I, who survived breast cancer and has been through all this before.
She was given a 30% chance to live for 5 years, too, and she's fully pushing it.
After that, you can consider yourself cured.

Hope to get my outside Christmas decorations up this weekend, before next week's chemo.

Subject: Re: Diana at Chemo ~ 17
11:45 pm, Thurs, Dec 5, 2013

Why does Carrie Underwood doing Sound of Music on TV strike me as odd yet sweet?
A classic of my youth has been repackaged for today's audiences, who have never seen a nun or a large unblended family.

Subject: Re: Diana at Chemo ~ 18
11:30 pm Fri, Dec 6, 2013

When I told my acupuncturist today how well I felt, she responded "but you've only had one treatment. Didn't they tell you what to expect?"
I know it's cumulative, but I feel like I weathered the first round of chemo so well, I should do OK with the next five. Plus, I have found that denial works very well for me.

I prefer to worry about whether Ukraine will really be bullied away from joining the EU by Putin, and whether my Lithuanian hero's, Gabrielė Petkevičaitė-Bitė's, historic home on St. Zita Street in Panevėžys will really be razed for McMansions. Plus, I am excited that weekend MARC service between DC and Baltimore starts tomorrow, and that the "Night of 100 Elvises" is in Baltimore tomorrow night.

I got to enjoy my firm's holiday party at the Ritz Carlton tonight, put on my red dress and pearls, and dance with others my age to "Stayin' Alive" and "I Will Survive." The associate attorneys preferred to linger demurely on the sidelines, guarding their young lawyer reputations in front of the partners. We older staff made the DJ's evening by requesting Motown.

I like walking home from the metro at midnight in the warm rain along my leafy street with its eclectic architecture and giant trees. I am thrilled we may have snow by Sunday.

Oh, and I still have my hair. If I don't tug at it, it seems to stay in.

Subject: Diana at Chemo ~ 19
6pm Sat, Dec 7, 2013

Primal and powerful – that's how my acupuncturist describes all belief traditions, and highly recommends adding them to one's cancer-combatting arsenal. So I am very grateful for everyone's prayers, thoughts, and transmittals of love. They are working.

He who sings prays twice, and our fearless carol-organizer, who is managing a very difficult bout of his own with colon/pancreatic cancer, pulled together a nice group of us from the listserv for a rehearsal at his home at 10 am this morning. We three sopranos, four altos, and three basses were so good (my main contribution is volume) that we were done in 45 minutes! The harmony is impressive. It also helps that a few of them sing professionally, and that we sing the same songs each year.

He and I discussed the two-pronged approach we have to take in our lives now — I won't die soon vs. I might die soon. Like the Country Western tune "Live like you are dying..." it's something to consider. But "keep calm and carry on" seems to be the best policy for now.

So carrying on the Christmas traditions, trying to get as much done as I can before doing chemo again next week: Christmas tree and pine roping bought, check. Fat colored bulbs hung on the big azalea bushes out front, check. Fence bedecked with red bows and white lights, not quite yet... We'll see what winter weather tomorrow brings...

Farewell, a long farewell to all my greatness!

Farewell, a long farewell to all my greatness!
This is the state of man: today he puts forth
The tender leaves of hope, tomorrow blossoms,
And bears his blushing honours thick upon him:
The third day comes a frost, a killing frost,
And - when he thinks, good easy man, full surely
His greatness is a-ripening - nips his root,
And then he falls, as I do.

William Shakespeare (1564-1616)
King Henry VIII, 1613[3]

Subject: Diana at Chemo ~ 20
11 pm Sun, Dec 8, 2013

I'll have to wear my wig tomorrow, so as not to scare people at work. Then I'll be off for the rest of the week as my second chemo is Tues-Wed-Thurs.

It's cold and icy outside and definitely feeling more like Christmas. Fence now bedecked with red bows and white lights. I have to have the house orderly by tomorrow night because my brother arrives Tuesday to be with me through this chemo, and then my daughter comes home for Christmas break on Friday.

I forget how I'll be feeling; the first chemo seems so long ago, three weeks. It was all so intense then, so many friends showering me with attention and love, making sure to take me there and back, and be with me through the night. It started as a frightening journey; now much less so. I am very fortunate.

Subject: Re: Diana at Chemo ~ 21
10 pm Mon, Dec 9, 2013

I have to take anti-nausea pills tonight, 12 hours and 6 hours before the taxol will be administered tomorrow. The infusion itself will start with hydration around 8 am tomorrow, with the heavy-duty stuff being introduced around 10 am, and then I stay connected until 5 pm. If things go as smoothly as they did the first time three weeks ago, I'll spend at least 4 hours of that time asleep.

Afterwards, I come home to a healthy meal cooked by one of those kale-loving millennials. My doctor told me today that I was anemic, and she will want to transfuse me should I drop below a certain number. I immediately ordered a roast beef sandwich and then cooked broccoli for dinner.

I am used to being a blood donor, and do not particularly relish being on the receiving end. I was once told that my blood was missing certain antibodies that made it perfect for newborns and premature babies. The Red Cross kept trying to get me to do a platelet donation, but the notion of having all my blood pumped out then pumped back into me again was unappealing. Nonetheless, it was disappointing when I learned that I could no longer donate blood, nor are my organs wanted anymore for transplant, nor my body for science. Cancer has tainted their value.

My wig got a lot of compliments today, and kept me warm in the wintry mix. Plus, being able to work for the past 6 days made me feel useful and normal.

Time to pack up my snacks and my reading materials and blanket (thank you, Nida!) and socks for tomorrow. On the way to a cure!

Subject: Re: Diana at Chemo ~ 22
Sun, Tues, Dec 10, 2013

After 9 hours of chemo, I could not feel better.

My brother is visiting from Ann Arbor. Friends made us a delicious dinner of kale and collards, grass-fed beef, Japanese sweet potatoes with butter from grass-fed cows, and dark chocolate for dessert. I added kale/fruit smoothies and cranberry kissel. Must admit, I prefer my kale blended raw with fruit.

My doctor mentioned I might consider radiation after chemotherapy, just for the area near the "vaginal cuff" where the lymph nodes were removed, just to be on the safe side. She would have recommended it even if I had let her do the more aggressive chemotherapy focusing on the rhabdo. I have read that radiation after chemo does not produce any measurable difference in carcinoma sarcoma cases. It's the rhabdo that's the wild card. Another thing I do not look forward to.

A young friend of mine in Baltimore, married only one year ago, has had to start radiation for non-Hodgkin lymphoma. Other than a child with cancer, there is nothing sadder than seeing a young adult with her life all ahead of her have to brave this.

Feeling guilty that my treatment seems so easy when that of others seem so difficult.

Subject: Diana at Chemo ~ 23
9:45 pm Wed, Dec 11, 2013

Mustard gas and yew, that's what they're putting into me. Ifosfamide and taxol.

But I feel okay. And a dinner of Shrimp Creole made by my brother was very welcome.

A young woman in her twenties is working remotely for HHS on fixing the Obamacare website while being infused in the chemo cubicle next to me. She has to be here five days a week once a month. She says she's pretty good until the fourth or fifth day.

A nice older gentleman was seated next to me toward the end of the day. Turns out he is Russian from Kyrgyzstan, and he and his daughter and I chatted in Russian for a long while. It was nice to realize that, when needed, I could resurrect the language I had studied at Indiana University in Bloomington.

And I got to meet a woman with a similar diagnosis to mine. Hers was discovered in May, and she's on a second chemo regimen. Hair has gone and come back. She's the one who told me about the mustard gas and taxol. They are treatments that have been around for 40 years.

Fading away now.

Subject: Re: Diana at Chemo ~ 24
10:45 pm Thur Dec 12, 2013

Felt a little shaky this morning but my 3rd chemo of the week went fine.
I needed a burger and fries afterwards.
Don't know why. Just did.

In the evening, my brother cooked a steak and potato dinner for four other friends and me, and we ate and drank and talked until after 10pm, on a school night.

The best my friends can do for me is treat me like everything is normal, and I love that they do.

Subject: Re: Diana at Chemo ~ 25
11:45 pm Fri, Dec 13, 2013

Friday the 13th, and my daughter arrived home safely from California.
Before turning in, we managed to cobble together a photo Christmas card, which will reach folks late, as usual...

Once we found out I had cancer, my daughter insisted on a photo shoot. We hired a local professional recommended by a neighbor, and he shot hundreds of stills of the two of us outside on a beautiful, windy late September day. I had just had my port installed that morning. You can read the anxiety in our faces. And the love.

My acupuncturist told me today that she could tell my liver was bearing the brunt of this last chemo, so that's what she focused on relieving. I visited her after getting my $5K shot of Neulasta on my own today, and even forgot to wear a mask on the metro.

It seems like the more I do, the more I can do.

Work was fine for one week. Starting Monday, I'll be doing it for two weeks at a stretch.

It may be time to go back to trying boot camp again. I feel like I have lost stamina and strength over the past three months and the only way to get that back is through exercise. After the new year, Vameka....

Because I Could Not Stop for Death (479) 1890
Emily Dickinson (1830-1886)[4]

Because I could not stop for Death,
He kindly stopped for me;
The carriage held but just ourselves
And Immortality.
We slowly drove, he knew no haste,
And I had put away
My labor, and my leisure too,
For his civility.
We passed the school, where children strove
At recess, in the ring;
We passed the fields of gazing grain,
We passed the setting sun.
Or rather, he passed us;
The dews grew quivering and chill,

For only gossamer my gown,
My tippet only tulle.
We paused before a house that seemed
A swelling of the ground;
The roof was scarcely visible,
The cornice but a mound.
Since then 'tis centuries, and yet each
Feels shorter than the day
*   I first surmised the horses' heads*
Were toward eternity.

Subject: Diana at Chemo ~ 26
11:00 pm Sat, Dec 14, 2013

Traditional 7am Saturday morning coffee with one of my oldest friends.

Then finished assembling a Christmas Eve vinaigrette (although mine is a variation that includes pickled beets, onions, Granny Smith apples, and garbanzo beans) for the Lithuanian Saturday School's Christmas pageant in Baltimore at 11am.

Sat at the Ambassador's table at the Lithuanian Hall and, with about 300 people, enjoyed a beautiful program of carols, songs, and dances, plus my favorite foods - mushrooms and herring.

I seriously considered attending what I knew would be a fabulous Christmas party this evening 38 miles away in Chantilly, VA, but opted for driving my daughter to a party across the Potomac River in Rosslyn before settling in for a long winter's nap. Still have to recover from those 19 hours of chemicals earlier this week. And there are carols to sing tomorrow.

Kitty has taken to sleeping with me again. She was wonderful after my operation, but kept her distance as soon as I started the chemo. My acupuncturist said she couldn't detect a chemical smell on me this week (it was kind of upsetting to me the first time she did!) so I guess Kitty does not either.

Subject: Diana at Chemo ~ 27
11:45 pm Sun, Dec 16, 2013

Posted our first three carols on Facebook. We sound good, if I do say so myself.

A young mother at Mass today in Georgetown told me not to fight the cancer, but to befriend it, accept it, and lead it out the door.

Another woman told me she had received a similar diagnosis, had the surgery, but refused the chemo. And she is fine several years later.

Well, I'm doing the chemo. But they all say the cure is in the mind.

I think I'm in a positive frame of mind, mainly because I just can't believe anything bad can really be happening to me.

So let's get back to Christmas. For over 25 years now we have gone to my good friends' home in Chevy Chase to help decorate their Christmas tree. I remember being so fascinated by their tree when I was still a newlywed — they made ornaments out of regular items that were meaningful to them. Over the years, I've tried to do the same. At one time, we all had babes in arms while decorating their tree. Now those children are all grown up and doing the decorating for us. Tradition!

Subject: Diana at Chemo ~ 28
5:30 pm Mon, Dec 16, 2013

The good thing about a wig is that it's like wearing a fur hat outside in the cold.
The bad thing about a wig is that it's like wearing a fur hat inside in the warmth.
Plus, it itches.
However, without it, when I comb out what little hair I have left, I look like a very white-skinned bald person with a blonde halo.

Tomorrow is my daughter's 23rd birthday and, blame it on learning I had cancer, I don't know what I was thinking months ago, but I bought her 4 tickets to Beyoncé at the Verizon Centre Wednesday night.
And now she wants me to go.
What 62-year old woman wants to go see Beyoncé?
I think it was the same spirit that propelled me to take my son to see the Rockettes at Radio City Music Hall right before my consult at Sloan Kettering and starting chemo at Sibley.
These are American cultural phenomena, and we should see them, at least once.

When I see pictures of snow falling in the Middle East, as is it doing now, I am so happy that I took my two adult children to Egypt over winter break in January 2011, returning just days before their Arab Spring.

Many of the interesting people on that trip, we found out at the end, were cancer survivors, and seeing Egypt had been on their "bucket list."

I guess I should start making a bucket list, too...

Or perhaps I'm just not imaginative enough. Staying employed and keeping my health insurance and being able to pay my expenses seems like a pretty lofty goal for me.

Subject: Re: Diana at Chemo ~ 29
11:00 pm Tues, Dec 17, 2013

My daughter finally found a good person to share her birthday with – the newly elected Pope Francis!
She'd long bemoaned having no one important born the same day as she was.
We were ecstatic upon visiting Kitty Hawk one summer to learn that the Wright Brothers had made their first flight on December 17th, 1903.

I made a cake from scratch in the morning and had hoped to serve grass-fed steaks (that one of my attorneys had brought in for me, along with beef liver) but my daughter preferred to order Roscoe's pizza and their arugula salad for some high school friends.

The Christmas tree is up and almost reaches our 10-foot ceiling. My daughter threaded white lights throughout so that it literally blazes. We hardly need ornaments.

Stopped at Nordstrom Rack downtown to check out knit caps to wear on my head at night.

I feel a twinge in my pelvic bones that is a result of the Neulasta shot taking effect and making my bone marrow produce.

Other than that, I am carrying on. Major decision: what to wear to tomorrow night's Beyoncé concert....

Subject: Re: Diana at Chemo ~ 30
11:30 pm, Wed, Dec 18, 2013

Beyoncé made me think of boot camp,
and how deeply I used to be able to do squats,
and how strong her core must be to be able to get down as low as she does.

Did not expect a Beyoncé concert to be so .... wholesome...
sexy, but in a classy way
Full of women's empowerment messages.
And sweet. Very, very loud, but sweet, and with incredible visuals.
I don't think I've seen so many happy people (and the Verizon Center was packed to the gills) since President Obama's first inauguration.

And we should all have a wind machine blowing our hair up and away from our faces.
My daughter insists Beyoncé rocks her weave, so I should feel better about my fake hair.

Had an acupuncturist appointment before the concert and managed a power nap on her table. She says she released a lot of chemical toxins from my body, but that they are going to town on all my organs.

Subject: Diana at Chemo ~ 31
11:30 pm Thur, Dec 19, 2013

I hope the swelling in my ankles is just due to having walked a mile home from the Silver Spring metro. It was a lovely warm winter night.

Working full time lends a structure to my day, and going, for example, to a reception at the Lithuanian Embassy afterward lets me mingle and network and feel engaged.

I am still inspired by the Beyoncé concert last night and happy to have my daughter (and her boyfriend) and soon my own son home from San Francisco for Christmas.

My firm has spent over $110,000 in medical expenses for me so far. My co-pays have amounted to almost $2,000, which seems like a pittance compared to what it could be. My firm uses Blue Cross/Blue Shield to administer the plan and get the discounts, and then they pay directly.

Recall the $5000 Neulasta shot I get at the conclusion of every chemo series? It's free for me. Here's another example: The Mesnex [Mesnex® (mesna) is a detoxifying agent to inhibit the hemorrhagic cystitis induced by ifosfamide (IFEX®)] costs $1,944.55 for 24 pills I take during the evenings after chemo. I pay $30 for them. They protect my bladder.

I am so glad I went for the HMO version of our Blue Cross Blue Shield Plan. I can't imagine having $5,000 or even

$1,000 in deductibles, or having insurance that covers only 80% of the rest. I'd be over $25,000 in debt by now if that were the case. Every week in chemo costs about $10,000. The costs seem out of control.

Here's a good video on the subject: http://www.youtube.com/watch?v=qSjGouBmo0M

Subject: Diana at Chemo ~ 32
10:47 am Sat Dec 21, 2013

I used to joke about being doomed to live a hundred years.
My father died at 92; my mother is alive and well at 90.
His mother lived to be 100.
I come from a long line of long-lifers.

With my particular diagnosis, however, I have a 35% chance of living 5 years.
That means a 65% chance of not.
Then again, many beat all odds and just keep on going for 17, 20, even more years.

My daughter got upset when I laughed at a TV commercial about the challenges of growing old.
"Guess I don't have to worry about that anymore!"
Not funny.

This whole thing is much harder on those who love us.
I would be going out of my mind if something like this had happened to either of my children.
But when you're the one going through it, you tend to forget the collateral damage.

Subject: Diana at Chemo ~ 33
10:30 pm Sat, Dec 21, 2013

There are so many winter solstice events taking place in my neighborhood tonight that, with the windows open to the 70 degree weather, I feel assaulted by voices from the party up the hill behind my house, the one next door, and the one I just came from across the street.

It is literally too loud with conversation outside for me to go to sleep.

The solstice event across the street included a description by Richard Harris of National Public Radio using a piece of wood and walking around a bonfire to show the tilt of the earth at both solstices and equinoxes. I ran into mothers from our Mother/Daughter book club of so many years ago, while serious musicians gathered in the studio to play serious folk music.

This is an interesting experience for my daughter and her boyfriend, because it is a very Baby Boomer kind of event. And so "Takoma." But it's the warm weather that has brought it to this strange intensity. I have never, even in summer, felt the voices of so many people partying come through my windows. Must be because there are no leaves to absorb the sound.

And so this is Christmas.....

Subject: Re: Diana at Chemo ~ 34
10:15 pm Sun, Dec 22, 2013

Found a sharp pair of scissors and snipped off what tufts were left on my head.
I am hacking and coughing with a cold (like a normal person!) so I had to pass on caroling at hospitals today.

Got bourbon balls made, and dough for cookies prepared. I.am.so.far.behind.

Plus, I am working full time this week.

It is so warm that I turned the heat off.

Going to bed now....

Subject: Re: Diana at Chemo ~ 35
11:00 pm Mon, Dec 23, 2013

The last thing I wanted to do today, after being treated to a Christmas lunch of Osso Bucco at the University Club by one of our attorneys, and realizing how much I still have to prepare for our Christmas eve dinner tomorrow night, was to go out to the Argentinian restaurant Fogo de Chao, for limitless meat.

But my son had arranged it with another family in the neighborhood, so I went along, figuring it was better to reinforce the nice idea rather than focus on how incredibly inconvenient it was for me.

But after getting home I read the results of my most recent blood work, and the nurse commented that I would probably have to get a blood transfusion with my next round of chemo next week.

Noooooooooooooooo! I do not want a blood transfusion! I've eaten grass-fed beef liver this week, as well as the meat just mentioned above. Surely my iron must be going up...

Subject: Re: Diana at Chemo ~ 36
10:30 pm Tues, Dec 24, 2013

What I neglected to mention in yesterday's post, and which a couple of people who get these emails brought to my attention, was that the evening that I so dreaded turned out to be wonderful.

I had known that the Mom of the family we were having dinner with was a poet, but learned that her son, my own son's friend, had tattooed a poem from someone his Mom and he both admire on his forearm:

Remember my little granite pail?
The handle of it was blue.
Think what's got away in my life —
Was enough to carry me thru.

Lorine Niedecker[5]

My son and a couple of these friends depart for Ireland December 26th on a tour that is enviably well arranged.

My daughter amazed everyone this Christmas Eve with her culinary skills. Our "Kūčios" was delicious and full of delicacies that I had never tasted ~ gourmet takes on the traditional 12-dish, meatless Lithuanian meal.

And the fact that my cards will not go out until Dec 26 does not seem so awful anymore.

Even now, after bowing out early to go to sleep in the downstairs guestroom, I can hear my daughter and her boyfriend and my son carrying on the evening with old family friends. They learned some Lithuanian traditions, and we got to know more about theirs.

My job is done.

Subject: Diana at Chemo ~ 37
11:00 pm Wed, Dec 25, 2013

If I had to worry about anything, it would be about this hacking and coughing.

At Christmas Mass today at 4:30 pm at the Shrine of the Immaculate Conception, that was my excuse for not sharing the sign of peace. Crossed my arms and inclined politely, "I have a cold."

My son gave me a watch for Christmas, an accessory I have not worn since cell phones told time, and my daughter gave me a turntable, which revived album after album from my basement. My children had never really heard music from vinyl! I had wonderful recordings of Bach, Mozart, Handel, and Van Cliburn's Tchaikovsky concert in Moscow. It was a quiet, magical Christmas Day. Dinner at the home of the friends we'd had over for Christmas Eve. Why is that delicious dough concoction called "Yorkshire Pudding?"

I am almost looking forward to my third chemo treatment next week. It is part of a ritual by now. I've given them my hair, and part of my continence. Now they want to give me blood, but I will resist.

Subject: Diana at Chemo ~ 38
11:30 pm Thur, Dec 26, 2013

I may never use outdated drugs again.
After a coughing fit that was so spasmodic I was choking and had tears running down my face (post-nasal drip has cursed me my entire life). I dug out a 2007-expired bottle of Delsym and chugged what was left in it.
That was around noon.
By the time I got to work at 1, by metro, I was feeling a little wobbly. My chest was red, my face was hot, and my lips a little numb. Thankfully, no one noticed, and it passed after a while. The unbalanced feeling was similar to how I react when they give me Benadryl among the first pre-meds in my chemo regimen. If I try to walk, I sway.

I thought the worst that could result from taking outdated medicine was that it would not work.
But it did. My cough magically disappeared. I think I just took too much.
I asked my daughter to drive me home, and all was well. How great to have her home from law school for Christmas Break!

Subject: Diana at Chemo ~ 39
8:30 pm Fri, Dec 27, 2013

A wonderful friend of mine offered to donate her own blood to me, even though she hadn't donated in a long time, and even called the hospital to see how to make the arrangements....

My oncologist said they don't make a practice of accepting designated blood. Processing has to be done through the Red Cross, involves a lot of paperwork, and doesn't always get to the intended recipient. She says designated donations, taking into account antibodies and other factors present in the blood, are often not so good a match as what the hospital arranges on its own. This is especially the case with family member donations.

But my red blood count remains in the normal zone (8.9). Healthy (enough to donate) is at 12. So long as I don't slide into the sevens, I can avoid a transfusion. What great friends I have, though!

Luckily, my oncologist also believes strongly in antibiotics and codeine, so good-bye spasmodic coughing…

Subject: Diana at Chemo ~ 40
11:30 pm Sat, Dec 28, 2013

Since I'm "doing so well" with the chemo, I asked my oncologist if we could just, well, quit it.
She chuckled.
They might consider stopping the chemo if I were truly debilitated by it but, since I'm "doing so well," they plan to

charge ahead with the full course in order to keep me "on the planet" longer. Two down, four to go.
Kale. One friend gave me "Fifty Shades of Kale," a cookbook, for Christmas.
Another friend stopped by today with fresh kale and sorrel from her garden.
This evening, got a gift of "Sautéed kale, chickpea & tomato braising sauce."

I am seeing pattern here.

Subject: Re: Diana at Chemo ~ 41
11:30 pm Sun, Dec 29, 2013

My niece and my daughter have been such great company~
They filled my pre-chemo day with museums, Ethiopian food, and "Saving Mr. Banks."
There's nothing more upbeat than being with Walt Disney's "Mary Poppins" again.

*"Winds in the east, mist coming in. / Like somethin' is brewin'
and bout to begin. / Can't put me finger on what lies in store, /
But I fear what's to happen all happened before."*

Subject: Re: Diana at Chemo ~ 42
8:00 pm Mon, Dec 30, 2013

Slept through most of the 9 hours of my chemo today, but am still tired.
Still thinking about the message in "Saving Mr. Banks" of creating something joyful from personal hurt, for both of them, Mr. Disney and Mrs. Travers.

And then I recalled the wonderful octogenarian, Oscar Shapiro, who lived in the Sedgwick Gardens on Connecticut Avenue before, while and after I lived there. He had never married or had children (and opined that it was easier for him to grow old alone, as he was already used to it!). But he threw a birthday party for himself every year at the old Roma Restaurant (3419 Connecticut Avenue with a full-sized stuffed bear at the entrance, now a Vietnamese restaurant), and I was somehow lucky enough to be treated with his many interesting friends.

The unfavored brother in a musical family (his brother was First Horn in the Boston Symphony Orchestra), Oscar worked at Western Union Telegraph until retirement, whereupon he became a full time chess master, traveling the world to play in simultaneous matches until he got beaten by a 12 year old.

He had also become a collector of Paganini memorabilia, now part of the Oscar Shapiro Collection of Paganinia; Oscar Shapiro Collection of Performing Arts Memorabilia in the New England Conservatory.

Oscar was a joy to be around, a kind chess master, and left a legacy in music, despite what his family thought about his lack of talent....

Subject: Diana at Chemo ~ 43
11:50 pm Tues, Dec 31, 2013

Happy New Year 2014 to all, and to all a good night!

Subject: Diana at Chemo ~ 44
10:15 pm Wed, Jan 1, 2014

Was 13 an unlucky number, 2013?
I don't think so.
My father died.
I got cancer.
But many good things happened, too.
Wesley was born.
The cancer is being chased away.
You write your own life story.

Subject: Diana at Chemo ~ 45
11:15 pm Thurs, Jan 2, 2014

Washington got a beautiful snowfall tonight.
Friends took me out for dinner.
My daughter is still here on her winter break.
My chemo is officially halfway done as of today.
All's right the world.

*"As if when on a winter's night you sit feasting with your
ealdormen and thegns, a single sparrow should fly swiftly into the
hall, and coming in at one door should instantly fly out through
another. In that time in which it is indoors it is indeed not touched
by the fury of winter, but yet, this smallest space of calmness being
passed almost in a flash, from winter going into winter again, it
is lost to your eyes. Somewhat like this appears the life of man; but
of what follows or what went before, we are utterly ignorant."*

**St. Bede, _Ecclesiastical History of the English People_, 731
AD. (672-735)**[6]

Subject: Re: Diana at Chemo ~ 46
11:15 pm Fri, Jan 3, 2014

Qigong and acupuncture in the afternoon to lessen the general feeling of yuckiness, not quite nausea, just queasiness from all of the chemicals dumped into my system this week.
Then, the Neulasta shot.
But the best medicine has been having my daughter around these past few weeks.
"The Wolf of Wall Street" left us both depressed.
She goes back to school on Sunday, and I have no more chemo for two weeks.
Thank goodness there's a weekend left.

Subject: Diana at Chemo ~ 47
11:30 pm, Sat, Jan 4, 2014

When my children were little and we'd drive past houses that were decorated in Christmas lights, they'd shout from the back seat, "Thank you! Thank you!"
I plug in my tree if I'm home during the day, because it's so beautiful.
I am glad it's dark and cold outside and the snow has turned to ice as the temperature dips down to zero tonight.
It makes the lights on my fence shine more brightly, and illuminates the sidewalk (at least until 1 am).
And when the thousands of cars pass my house coming back from work at 4:30 pm this week, the lights will still come on, and maybe the motorists will feel a little bit of the same joy my children felt when it was dark outside and suddenly they were greeted by Christmas lights.

Subject: Diana's Detour ~ 48
11:00 pm Sun, Jan 5, 2014

A friend suggested I change the name of this blog to "Diana's Journey."
I thought "Detour" was more fitting.
I don't intend to go anywhere other than off the beaten path for a while.

Without my hair, I look like ET, but I don't show anyone.
When someone compliments me on my new hairdo, I don't laugh anymore and say, "Oh, it's a wig. I have cancer."
That's jolting and upsetting. People don't need that information.
I want to get over this and not have it become my identity.

Tomorrow is Epiphany, the Feast of the Three Kings/Magi/Wise Men, Twelfth Night.
I'm not ready for Christmas to be over yet, and am fine with extending the season to as many as forty days, ending on Candlemas (February 2).
But off to two weeks of work!

Subject: Diana's Detour ~ 49
9:45 pm, Mon, Jan 6, 2014

The wind has stopped howling; now I guess the temperature is quietly dropping. Oops, the wind has picked up again.

My 90-year old mother moved into a fancy retirement home today, in the coldest weather possible in Cincinnati.

My older brother blew a tire getting there from Ann Arbor to help, making it an 8-hour trip. Drove back today on black ice.
My younger brother made most of the arrangements, and did most of the hand-holding.
A designer had come in and surveyed her home, determined her style, selected which pieces would fit.
A few hours after leaving her home, my mother moved into an edited version of it.

Learned about Kombucha tonight, and about Finnish vili (a yoghurt-like food which really does have a texture I have not seen before — viscous, almost jelly-like). My mother used to make her own yoghurt, back in the 1960s, on a square warming plate with four square covered glass cups. That was before yoghurt was cool. It was a European health thing.

Subject: Diana's Detour ~ 50
10:45 pm, Wed, Jan 7, 2014

One friend insists on driving me to the metro when it's 7 degrees outside, although I can walk the quarter mile perfectly well.
She says this is her year of living purposefully, after 30 years of teaching French in middle school.

Another invites me to visit Longwood Gardens with her this Sunday where it will be 54 degrees outside.
She knows my weak spot. I've already been eyeing the Philadelphia Flower Show.

This summer I hope to grow lots of garlic, scallions, leek, parsley, cilantro, and dill.
I usually have so little success that I should focus on plants I really need to eat,
not wonder at the squash that takes over my driveway but refuses to fruit or worry over the tomatoes that grow tall and leafy but produce nothing.

Arugula I can grow, so I should.

And something for the birds, butterflies and bees, too.

Subject: Diana's Detour ~ 51
11:30 pm, Wed, Jan 8, 2014

I'm not supposed to deal with kitty litter, but what am I going to do the night before trash day?
I put on a mask and rubber gloves and deal with it.

I'm also not supposed to get manicures or pedicures, but I went ahead with my daughter and we got ours before she left.
Before that, I was already feeling a little tingling in my fingers and toes, but very little.
They said neuropathy was a possible side effect of the chemo. So far, it's very minor.

I'm also not supposed to have any dental work done, but I wonder if that includes regular teeth cleaning (I learn it does, and have to postpone).

And as far as the ban on gardening goes, I'll have to deal with that the way I did with kitty litter.
I think the greatest concern is picking up bacteria from bare earth.

Like toxoplasmosis. Here I'll mention a pet peeve of mine — people who allow their cats outside.
I attract birds to my yard with suet and water, and protect them from my own cat, an accomplished predator, by keeping her inside. But that just means those lovely flying creatures fall prey to neighboring felines. They enjoy a hunt I deny my own.

From an NYT article in January 2013

Fluffies that spend part of the day outdoors and the unnamed strays and ferals that never leave it — kill a median of 2.4 billion birds and 12.3 billion mammals a year, most of them native mammals like shrews, chipmunks and voles rather than introduced pests like the Norway rat.

I'll end now.

Subject: Diana's Detour ~ 52
Thurs, Jan 9, 2014

A "neatnik" friend of mine came over this evening to help me pull out some clothes for donation.
I have a tendency to hold onto too much stuff.

I also have a sentimental attachment to any clothing that someone I cared for has given to me.
We went through closets and suitcases of clothes, and filled two giant Ikea bags.

I used to think that one useful tactic to get rid of clutter was to pretend to have only six months to live.
That would be a good motivation to clear things out so as not to leave a mess for your family.

It didn't work, not even when it's more a probability than a possibility.

Little by little though, if only for the purpose of living lighter...

Subject: Diana's Detour ~ 53
10:45 pm, Fri, Jan 10, 2014

People at work are so kind.
I've worked here, off and on, since 1996.
There is a lot of shared everydayness, weathering of crises, surviving layoffs.

Most often I get looks of surprise, and then a little confusion. From the managing partner to the mailroom staff, they have probably heard that I have cancer, and are a little shocked to see me at work at all, much less looking normal (but with a Tina Turner hairstyle).

Most people don't say anything, unless they have something to say.

And then it's words of friendship and support, and encouragement, and love.

On the elevator one day, a senior partner bent down and whispered to me "I'll be praying for you."

The receptionist told me today that she was a breast cancer survivor.
She gave me a website that helps her find faith in God.
We have something intimate in common.

She assured me that good comes out of this experience.
"It's just God getting your attention!" she's convinced.

Sent: Tue, Jan 14, 2014 12:41 am
Subject: Re: Diana's Detour ~ 55
10:00 pm Mon, Jan 13, 2014

Earlier to bed tonight. Too few hours slept last night.

It's a beautiful carousel we're on.
We get a good number of spins on it, and then we're off.
It twirled before us, and will keep on twirling without us,
Oblivious that we're gone.

But we got to ride!

Subject: Diana's Detour ~ 54
11 pm Sat, Jan 11, 2014

"The priest just hurt himself playing basketball and went to the hospital."

"So he won't be able to say Mass this afternoon."
"Oh, he'll be there."

And he was.

The Lithuanian community has a new priest in town, and he's a diplomat from the Papal Nuncio (Vatican Embassy). A quiet, serious late 30-ish man who's thrown himself into the community wholeheartedly.
To the extent that we find him playing basketball Saturday morning with the Dads who've brought their kids to Lithuanian Saturday school.

Spending an overcast winter day with the creative and energetic folks from this community shores me up, gives me energy, makes me want to do more. At home alone, I might have cleaned house, pored over seed catalogues, taken down Christmas decorations ~ all good things, just not quite so inspiring. I need to be inspired to keep on keeping on.

Subject: Re: Diana's Detour ~ 55
11:11 pm, Sun, Jan 12, 2014

I've decided that it's time to move back home, that is, out of the downstairs guest room, and back upstairs to my own bedroom.

I used the excuse of a friend of a friend who needed a place to spend the night to return to my old room-at-the-inn ways. And I wasn't disappointed.
Guests like this are always a delight, unfailingly polite, and we spend hours talking.

And this after a brisk winter day of taking in the beauty of Longwood Gardens in Delaware and its fanciful horticultural displays in the company of an old friend.

Throw in a two-hour board meeting conducted via telephone in between, and I feel positively re-charged.
The tree will have to wait until tomorrow after work to be taken down...

Subject: Diana's Detour ~ 56
Mon, Jan 13, 2014

Caught up on Downton Abbey via a PBS rerun tonight, and highlights of last night's Golden Globes online. My guilty pleasures last year were "Breaking Bad" and "Orange is the New Black." "Breaking Bad" lends the innocent little bell on my table at chemo a sinister aspect…

Subject: Diana's Detour ~ 57
11:15pm Tues, Jan 14, 2014

My acupuncturist told me today I was doing fantastically.
"But you said you've never treated anyone getting my particular chemicals."
"I read up about it," she replied.

Other than drowsiness from reading at night when I can't sleep, I'm feeling fine.
It's that sense of well-being one gets right before the next dose of chemo.
I hope to deny myself right into a cure.

Subject: Diana's Detour ~ 58
10:45 pm, Wed, Jan 15, 2014

The moon is full.
Temperature is dropping.
Winter is back.

Getting things ready.
Last day at work tomorrow until January 27.

Three chemos down, three to go.
Does that make the glass half empty or half full?

Subject: Diana's Detour ~ 59
10:00 pm, Thurs, Jan 16, 2014

I never regret making the effort to go to a concert after work
in the middle of the week.
Came home at 10pm from another beautiful musical event
at the Lithuanian Embassy.
So many people attended. What talent and great company
we got to enjoy.

I am never so happy as when I am planning a major event.
I have learned not to be afraid to reach high.
I invited Zbigniew Brzezinski to be our keynote speaker at
Independence Day in mid-February.
I also recognize when to use contacts, so I went through the
Embassy.
He responded immediately, with deep regret that his
calendar was full.
But he responded! How cool is that!

My acupuncturist told me that the reason I was doing so well is because I am staying engaged.
She may be right.
I prefer going full speed as if nothing is wrong.

There's a Russian verb "to scatter energy in many directions." I've always operated that way. It may not be the most efficient way to live, but it works well enough for me.

Subject: Diana's Detour ~ 60
10:00 pm Fri, Jan 17, 2014

Had my half-way through chemo scan today, and it's all clear!
Barium drink, iodine drip, back and forth through the donut hole scan machine, and results within the hour.

My doctor went through her list of possible side effects, most of which I continue *not* to have.
She said it was good I'd lost my hair; otherwise she'd have doubts whether I was really getting the chemo.

Three more sessions of chemo, and then we're done, in mid-March.
She talked about getting scans every three months for two years after that.

We talked about removing the port at that point, how some people keep theirs in as a talisman to ward off the return of any cancer, but you have to get it flushed every month to prevent blood clots in that case. No mention of radiation.

I went home and fell asleep for four hours.

Subject: Re: Diana's Detour ~ 61
11:30 pm, Sat, Jan 18, 2014

During conversation after a dinner party tonight, I was texted a sketch of the Golden Gate bridge that my daughter was drawing, sharing a sunset moment with me.

I realize the most precious things we offer or leave behind are those that we create, not what we acquire.

I think of the starched white table runners of reinforced cut embroidery (Hardanger) that my grandmother made. I've managed to stash away a few.

The oil pastel painted by the father of my late Danish sister-in-law hangs in my kitchen. He is gone. She is gone.

Time to get creative...

Subject: Diana's Detour ~ 62
11:15 pm, Sun, Jan 19, 2014

I love hearing from new people about old history.
Met two lovely youngish aged sisters tonight who described in incredible detail wartime events from 1941 when they were little girls. Such sharp minds. Such full lives.

What is it about January that makes me want to start seeds indoors? It's much too early. Anything that I get to sprout now will be way too leggy before it's time to put outside. So I've decided I will just test out the viability of old seeds on moist paper towels in plastic sandwich bags. Everything from feoniculum to aquilegia. Including those palm tree seeds I've been saving from my late mother-in-law's house in Florida... from twenty years ago.

Subject: Diana's Detour ~ 63
10pm Mon, Jan 20, 2014

In honor of the Martin Luther King holiday, I went to see "12 Years a Slave."
Moving, depressing, have we really made much progress since then ...

Preparing for tomorrow's snow. My car's been pulled off the street and parked in the driveway.
My ride to chemo should be fine, but getting home might require something other than another friend driving in from Virginia to give me a ride.

Subject: Diana's Detour ~ 64
10:15 p Tues, Jan 21, 2014

Schools and the federal government may close down, but hospitals stay open! And good friends get me there for my chemo.

Which went fine again today. The port is your best friend. One painless prick and for three days I get hydrated, sedated, protected with anti-nauseals, protected against any allergic reactions, and then poisoned ~ by my ever pleasant, calm and competent nurse Natasha. She brings me water and cranberry juice and a sandwich from the Au Bon Pain downstairs, while constantly attaching and removing new bags of infusions.

They don't do just cancer treatments here. Many people come in for transfusions, hydrations, and other IV administered drugs. I was the first there today, and almost the last to leave. The snow may have kept some regulars away, but Natasha claims she will be there no matter what.

Apropos of yesterday's message.
A president's limited power to effect change: Obama said that even the greatest presidents — like Abraham Lincoln — had to operate in the currents of history. [I]t took another hundred and fifty years before African-Americans had anything approaching formal equality, much less real equality. .... [A]t the end of the day we're part of a long-running story. We just try to get our paragraph right.

And must mention that when I got home today, I found that my stairs and sidewalks had been shoveled by kind neighbors...
Thank-you!

Subject: Diana's Detour ~ 65
9:30 pm, Wed, Jan 22, 2013

Second day of chemo is ruddy and puffy day. Instead of sleeping the day away I worked on my Lithuanian community matters. Drafted a letter to President Obama re Ukrainian protests and the Sochi Olympics. Finalized speakers and logistics for the Independence Day celebration. Before I knew it, the five hours were over.

Distracted myself afterward with a visit to the recycled household goods site called Community Forklift and a movie. Interesting to see "Inside Llewyn Davis" on the same day as the 41st anniversary of Roe v. Wade and the March for Life on the Mall.

I am happy to report that some seeds have already sprouted in the sandwich bags!

- 2012 Hollyhock
- 2011 Bulls Blood Beet
- 2008 Fennel

I am thinking of visiting Arizona once this is all over in April. There's a wedding in Phoenix I want to attend, and I want to build in a few days to see a friend in Sedona and perhaps visit some Indian mesas. I hear it's a place of magical healing. And from having driven cross-country twice, I know it's beautiful.

Subject: Diana's Detour ~ 66
10:30 pm, Thurs, Jan 23, 2013

Linked-In advised people that today was my 18th year of working at the law firm.
I got to re-connect with someone I hadn't spoken to in years.
Hard to believe how a job that was supposed to be a stopgap measure turns into a life.

I keep thinking I'm fine until I get home and I don't feel so fine.
Which made receiving a personally delivered home-roasted chicken from a friend so precious.
I ate some, and then slept the afternoon away.

Visiting Arizona is looking more and more like a great way to celebrate the end of all this.

Subject: Diana's Detour ~ 67
9:30 pm, Fri, Jan 24, 2014

It was so blazingly bright today on the remaining snow; we're not used to such days in winter.

Not used to snow staying around on the ground at least, or cold for such a long time.

Taking the metro to my 9 am acupuncturist appointment at Dupont Circle, the rail yards near Union Station seemed like a scene from the movie "Dr. Zhivago."

I really needed the acupuncture this morning; it made me feel better, and that's its purpose, to help with the effects of the chemo. Getting there on my own was fine, but I much appreciated a friend of mine giving me a ride to the hospital in the afternoon for my Neulasta shot.

And then all I wanted to do was be alone. To recover at my own pace. And tonight I feel better already.

Subject: Diana's Detour ~ 68
10:45 pm, Sat, Jan 25, 2014

Blame it on those two years we lived in Southern California, but come Oscar season, I feel obliged to see as many of the nominated films as possible. Tonight it was "Nebraska." Filmed in black and white on location, and focusing on adult family dynamics, many of whose members are over 70; who knew it could be so interesting?

I did not make it to the Lithuanian Saturday school today. I opted for the anti-nauseal drugs I had not used yet instead.

I was just impatient about feeling lousy. After the movie, went for a burger and fries and a beer at McGinty's with a friend. It made me feel better.

Facebook is fabulous for keeping us informed about minute-by-minute developments in Ukraine. Compared to Syria and Egypt and the Columbia mall shooting today, news about Ukraine seems to have fallen by the wayside.

Facebook also provided a link to a You Tube film about Lithuania's pre-eminent painter and composer, Mikalojus Čiurlionis, entitled "Letters to Sofia." Beautiful. While watching it on the computer, I posted about it to the 700 members on our Lithuanian community listserv that it was a "Lithuanian Downton Abbey." A couple of hours later, I got an email from one of the film's producers in Lithuania railing at me that the You Tube was a piracy and not to show it. Which I wasn't doing anyway, just publicizing it. He later apologized profusely, said he was stuck in a bus filming in freezing cold temperatures in Vilnius, and had become incensed when someone informed him that his Čiurlionis film was being shown for free online. The life of an artist is a constant struggle. Now I am one of his supporters.

Subject: Diana's Detour ~ 69
10:30 pm, Sun, Jan 26, 2014

Did not expect to find Sherlock (Benedict Cumberbatch) in the film "August: Osage County." He's little Charlie. Not quite sure what to make of that movie. Taking the high road and being strong brings no love. Giving up and getting away is the only way forward.

I keep being shown attention and offered rides and given flowers and food and clothing. And all this because of a dread disease. I don't feel like I deserve it. People are just incredibly nice.

And then I realized there are rules for this. And I have been the beneficiary of many who may not have even heard of them.

Corporal Works of Mercy

Corporal Works of Mercy are those that tend to bodily needs of others. In (Matthew 25:34-40, in The Judgment of Nations six specific Works of Mercy are enumerated, although not this precise list — as the reason for the salvation of the saved, and the omission of them as the reason for damnation. The last work of mercy, burying the dead, comes from the Book of Tobit.

1. *To feed the hungry.*
2. *To give drink to the thirsty.*
3. *To clothe the naked.*
4. *To harbour the harbourless. (also loosely interpreted today as To Shelter the Homeless)*
5. *To visit the sick.*
6. *To visit the imprisoned (classical term is "To ransom the captive")*
7. *To bury the dead.*

Spiritual Works of Mercy

Though ideally applicable for all faithful, not everyone is considered capable or obligated to perform the first three spiritual works of mercy if they do not have proper tact, knowledge or canonical training to do so. The last four works are considered to be an obligation of all faithful to practice unconditionally.

1. *To instruct the ignorant.*
2. *To counsel the doubtful.*
3. *To admonish sinners*
4. *To bear wrongs patiently.*
5. *To forgive offences willingly.*
6. *To comfort the afflicted.*
7. *To pray for the living and the dead.*

Subject: Diana's Detour ~ 70
11:45 pm, Mon, Jan 27, 201

There was nothing like going to afternoon Mass yesterday and having someone you saw grow up, now with his own business and his own family and, though very conservative politically does everything organically, offer to get you some pot to help with the nausea.

I don't want to smoke anything because it would make me cough, but I was told cannabis can be blended into butter or a spread. How sweet! I'll let him know if I ever need it.

So glad to be back at work today. Two more weeks of normalcy. Four chemos down, two to go.

Subject: Diana's Detour ~ 71
10:30 pm, Tues, Jan 29, 2014

Have to admit, I love our President. He did a great job with the State of the Union speech tonight...

A young Lithuanian student who once lived with me asked, after watching Obama and McCain debating, "Why do they always end with 'God bless America?' America has already been so blessed..." He also believed that, "of course, McCain should be president, not that 'simple black man.'"

Now back to my detour... my older brother called yesterday and told me that, just as the effect of the chemicals in my body is cumulative, so too would be the effectiveness of anti-nauseals, and I should be taking them before I feel awful. It's not that I feel nauseated; it's just that sometimes I don't feel great, and I want to bounce back and feel great immediately.

Soooo cold today. Schools in Chicago and Detroit were closed. And the South is getting slammed.

Subject: Diana's Detour ~ 72
10 pm Wed, Jan 29, 2014

I wish I knew how long I was going to live. I think all of us would.
It would make figuring out when, or if, to retire so much easier.

At 62, I could take the lower Social Security amounts now, but if I continue to work, $1 is deducted from my benefit payments for every $2 I earn above the annual limit of about $15,000. But if I didn't work, what would I do?

At 66, I would be at "full retirement age," could get full SS benefits and continue to earn as much as I like, but will I make it that long?

At 70, which is how long I had planned to work, the monthly SS payments would be a lot more. But that is when I counted on living to be 100.

At 88, it all seems to break even, no matter which option you choose: retiring early, on time, or extended.

77 is 15 more years of life, which is way more than my diagnosis allows, but it's also the basic lifespan of an American.

However, according to the Social Security Administration, a woman turning age 65 today can expect to live, on average, until age 86.

So I should plan on making it to at least 77, like a normal American?

But if I make it to 65, I can count on making it to 86... sounds good to me.

Subject: Diana's Detour ~ 73
11pm, Thur Jan 30, 2014

One very sweet colleague expressed concern when I sent around a message saying I was leaving early at 5pm.

"Is everything all right?"

"Oh, sure, I am just going to the Kennedy Center tonight."

Once again, I am showered with blessings from friends. A three-part concert at the Kennedy Center.

Why do I not go there more often? An amazing performance of Mendelssohn by violinist Joshua Bell, then an hour-long Hindemith requiem to the words of Walt Whitman's "When Lilacs Last in the dooryard bloom'd" with a baritone, a mezzo, and the Choral Arts Society of Washington, DC. And then something called a "postlude" after the concert, when the audience gets to leave or can opt to stay and listen to an additional program of organ music. We stayed, of course.

I found the words Whitman had written on the death of Lincoln to be beautiful, not morbid...

Prais'd be the fathomless universe,
For life and joy, and for objects and knowledge curious,
And for love, sweet love—but praise! praise! praise!
For the sure-enwinding arms of cold-enfolding death.
...
Over the tree tops I float thee a song,
Over the rising and sinking waves, over the myriad fields and
*   the prairies wide,*
Over the dense-pack'd cities all and the teeming wharves and
*   ways,*
I float this carol with joy, with joy to thee, o Death.

"When Lilacs Last in the Dooryard Bloom'd", Walt Whitman (1819–1892) in 1865.[7]

Subject: Diana's Detour ~ 74
9:45 pm, Friday, Jan 31, 2014

It's the Chinese New Year, and it's the Year of the Horse.
This didn't mean anything to me until I realized that my
little girl is a horse in Chinese astrology!
And we share an element ~ "metal."

My son, it turns out, is the snake sign. His element is earth.

Their father is a rooster. His element is wood.

And me, I'm a rabbit.
My acupuncturist thought I might be a dragon.
Far from it.

Subject: Diana's Detour ~ 75
8:00 pm, Sat, Feb 1, 2014

You know it's been a cold winter in Washington, DC when
you don't see a Snowdrop bloom until February.
They're usually out and about in December.
But I saw one this morning shyly poking out its white petals
from a tiny tuft of green.
Small in size, but no wonder: this just in from our local
listserv:

*The National Weather Service has issued a WINTER STORM
WATCH for MontgomeryCounty from Sunday night through
Monday. Snowfall of 5 inches or more is possible.*

My acupuncturist expressed a little skepticism about the
steroid combo I had been given as an anti-nauseal, and I

confirmed it does seem to interfere with my sleep. She noted that my stomach was still unhappy from the chemotherapy despite them. I have alternatives to try (Compazine, Atavan...) .

I have also decided to switch my radio diet from non-stop NPR "All things considered" to classical music. Has anyone ever prescribed this? Incredibly calming.

It just means abandoning my responsibility to constantly worry about the world...

Subject: Re: Diana's Detour ~ 76
10:30 pm, Sun, Feb 2, 2014

Super Bowl Sunday, Groundhog Day, Candlemas.

It turns out that Candlemas Day is the precursor to Groundhog Day. And it has been celebrated for at 2,000 years.
Why? Because it just so happens that Feb. 2 is the halfway point between the winter solstice — a.k.a., shortest day of the year — and the spring equinox.
But there's more. Candlemas became the day for blessing candles that were to be used in the church during the coming year. It also happens to be 40 days since Christmas, (have you put the decorations away yet?) so Candlemas became the traditional Christian feast day to commemorate Mary's purification ritual following the birth of Jesus, as well as the presentation of Jesus at the temple.
Sometime early in the 16th century, Candlemas Day evolved into a day when German farmers tried to get a feel for how the oncoming growing season may go, Casteel said. The farmers would look for animals that hibernated — hedge hogs were

popular in Europe — to see if they were stirring. They determined that seeing a shadow Feb. 2 meant a longer winter, while cloudy skies indicated an early spring.
When Europeans settled North America, they brought their Feb. 2 tradition. But there are no hedge hogs here, Casteel pointed out, so the farmers started checking on groundhogs.
Of course, the whole thing became commercialized in 1886 with Punxsutawney Phil.

Pruned some roses and the butterfly bush. Bought some more seeds. Enjoyed a barbecue dinner at friends for the football game, switching to *Downton Abbey* after half time...

I actually went to our regular parish today, and the visiting priest turned out to be interesting. He'd spent time in Russia (Khabarovsk) and speaks Russian. How did he wind up at St. Bernadette's in Silver Spring? Even told a joke: Seems a monastery in England was running low on funds and needed to generate some revenue. One person suggested the priests could bake bread. Someone else proposed they make brandy. They finally settled on the idea of a fish and chips place. That venture proved so successful it was drawing customers from near and far. Someone asked, "Are you the fish Friar?" No, I'm the chip Monk...."

Subject: Re: Diana's Detour ~ 77
9:00 pm Mon, Feb 3, 2014

I found a box of paperwhites on my doorstep when I got back from work today. Thank you!
What a soggy day. But I believe in giant umbrellas. They make walking in the rain a delight.

I just had my whole line-up for our Lithuanian Independence Day program on Sunday, Feb 16th, turned upside down.
Glad I hadn't sent out the hard-copy invites yet. Procrastination saves the day again.
Have to remember to order the raguolis/šakotis (baumkuchen ~ a tree cake) from Connecticut this week.

A lot of things happening next week, while I have chemo.
Gala Wednesday night, after my second day. I said I'd go, although I may be red and puffy.
Had hoped to make a quick trip up to NYC on Thursday afternoon for a seminar on Yiddish Lithuania, after my third day.
I may have to pass on that.
Big event on Sunday, for one hundred, perhaps two hundred people.
I should be OK by then.

Subject: Diana's Detour ~ 78
11:30 pm, Tues, Feb 4, 2014

My main speaker for Independence Day informed me that he has cancer, too, leukemia. He pumps his own every evening, and will have to for the rest of his life.
So many people have this. It's almost the new normal.

Olympics starting in Sochi on Thursday.
Lots of hope in the air.

Subject: Diana's Detour ~ 79
11:45 pm Wed, Feb 5, 2014

Sometimes it's a toss-up.
Is that my fur hat, my wig, or the cat on the chair?

Subject: Diana's Detour ~ 80
11:55 pm, Thurs, Feb 6, 2014

My daughter sent me this.

I Live My Life In Ever Widening Rings (from The Book of
Hours)[8]

I live my life in ever widening rings
that embrace the simple things around me.
Perhaps I'll never reach them all,
but I'm going to try.
I've been circling around God, around this ancient tower.
I've been circling this way for thousands of years.
And I still don't know: am I a falcon, or a storm,
or some great song?

— *Rainer Maria Rilke (1875-1926) 1905*
Translated from German by Paul Weinfield, © 2014

Subject: Re: Diana's Detour ~ 81
Fri, Feb 7, 2014 11:21 pm

I liked the poem my daughter sent me yesterday so much
that I checked out what Garrison Keillor had in his Writers
Almanac this morning. His broadcast comes on each

morning at 6:45am on our National Public Radio station, but I also get it sent to my inbox. I particularly liked the title.

Our Ground Time Here Will Be Brief[9]

Blue landing lights make
nail holes in the dark.
A fine snow falls. We sit
on the tarmac taking on
the mail, quick freight,
trays of laboratory mice,
coffee and Danish for
the passengers.
Wherever we're going
is Monday morning.
Wherever we're coming from
is Mother's lap.
On the cloud-packed above, strewn
as loosely as parsnip
or celery seeds, lie
the souls of the unborn:
my children's children's
children and their father.
We gather speed for the last run
and lift off into the weather.

—Maxine Kumin

Subject: Re: Diana's Detour ~ 82
11:30 pm Sat, Feb 8, 2014

I tend to avoid housekeeping at all costs.

Would much rather be networking with parents at the Saturday school, then later with those attending mass in the afternoon at the National Shrine. Prayer power must have been working because during that mass I missed calls from my son, my daughter, a friend from Palo Alto, and an old friend who wound up taking me out for a movie and dinner tonight.

The house was still there when I got home.

Red blood count good. No transfusions needed. Two days left to get everything done before the next chemo.

Subject: Diana's Detour ~ 83
10pm, Sun, Feb 10, 2014

All it takes is one car recklessly crossing into your lane on the beltway to make you realize how quickly things could end. Who needs a scary diagnosis when a stupid girl from New Jersey not paying attention could be so much worse.

So I am starting a binder. Just in case. Because it will be needed, sooner or later.

How does a TIAA-CREF retirement account get paid out?
Would my children get a check for half each?
Would it be taxed? How quickly does it come? Is it for the entire amount?
And life insurance. All things a will doesn't cover.

And now there is the digital audit. So many passwords. So many log-ins. So many codes.

I have been so lucky all my life. Not even a broken bone.
Never injured in a car accident.
Hope my luck is not running out.

Subject: Diana's Detour ~ 84
11pm, Mon, Feb 10, 2014

"Cancer becomes you!" was the gist of a compliment I received the other evening. I hadn't seen this person in about a year, and I'm sure he meant well. "You've lost some weight... love the hair."

If only he could see me with a black turtleneck minus the wig. I look like Uncle Fester from the Addams Family.

Have to get some sleep. Early chemo tomorrow.

Subject: Diana's Detour ~ 85
11:30 pm, Tues, Feb 11 2014

It seems that every time I have gone to chemo recently, I bring the threat of a snowstorm with me.
One nurse is married to a meteorologist who claims the snow coming tomorrow night is going to be serious.
And my oncologist has actually raised the possibility of moving my Thursday treatment to Friday, if need be.

Today is the 50th anniversary of the Beatles appearing (during a snowstorm!) in Washington, DC. I was invited to a tribute concert at the Coliseum, but it would have involved standing for 5 hours, so I decided to pass.

Shirley Temple died today. Now that was a life.

The first day of chemo, though 9 hours long, is fine. The Benadryl knocked me out for 4 hours. Then I got to talking with other patients.

I heard Andrew in the next cube talking about how blessed he was that it was easier for him than others, so I had to ask. Seems he had colon cancer that jumped to his liver. This is his second round of chemo, as the cancer came back like rice pellets spread throughout his peritoneum. He was given one year to live until his family found a clinical trial with a Dr. Sugarbaker. The new method involved neck to navel opening, picking out each rice-sized pellet of cancer, and then doing a hot chemo wash. Apparently it worked. Something still shows up in the liver, but you can get by with only 35% of your liver.

"Dr. Sugarbaker was a colleague of my husband's" piped up a patient who strolled over from another cubicle. This short-haired (it's growing back) tiny woman about my age remarked on the irony of her being married to surgeon specializing in carcinoma sarcoma and then getting the disease herself in her chest cavity. But her pride is a 5 foot S-shaped scar. She is athletic. Andrew is a triathlete.

I am in good company.

Subject: Re: Diana's Detour ~ 86
11:30 pm, Wed, Feb 12, 2014

Someone shoveled my steps!
The snow is supposed to come down hard after midnight.
Schools are closed for tomorrow, and so is my office.
Will see about getting to chemo.
Going to bed now.

Subject: Re: Diana's Detour ~ 87
11:45 pm, Thurs, Feb 13, 2014

My nurse called early this morning to say that their staff could not get out of their own driveways, so my chemo would be postponed until Friday.

Outside was a winter wonderland. Fluffy dry snow on top of a snowman-worthy layer.

I didn't go out to shovel until around 10 am, and I did that mostly to be out in the fresh air, another antidote to feeling queasy. I got most of it done, but my neighbors finished the driveway apron.

Schools are closed tomorrow, too. It snowed some more tonight, but I think I'll be able to get to chemo tomorrow with the help of a friend in the neighborhood.

Wish I'd gotten more done today, but slept a lot, then got busy on the computer in the evening. Sometimes, I let myself cave in to the temptation to sleep.

Subject: Diana's Detour ~ 88
10:30 pm, Fri, Feb 14, 2014

There was a beautiful full moon out tonight, this Valentine's Day.

We are totally at the mercy of the weather.
Snow is expected tomorrow now.
So Saturday school was called off and the kids' celebration moved onto my Sunday Independence Day program.
I have just guaranteed 100 people minimum for Sunday brunch, and can only hope that the snow passes by then.

It was so icy this morning that I called a local car service rather than risk my friend's bringing me in.
By the afternoon, however, it was warming up.
Taking a day off between infusions 2 and 3 this week made me feel better.
But I really craved, and indulged in, a Big Mac and fries after it was over.

Then acupuncture, which I think is like have little chimneys poked into your body to allow the toxins to escape.

Subject: Diana's Detour ~ 89
10:30 pm, Sat, Feb 15, 2014

Despite predictions, there was no snow today, but a cold wind has picked up tonight.
It doesn't look like it'll get above freezing tomorrow.
And I'm afraid that might keep people away from the Lithuanian Independence Day celebration.

I got my copying done at Kinko's.
And picked up yellow and red carnations at the grocery store for the kids to carry in during Mass at St. Matthew's Cathedral tomorrow.

I passed a neighbor shoveling snow, and she asked if I'd been to the beach.
I guess the ruddy and puffy sometimes looks tan.

Subject: Diana's Detour ~ 90
11:45 pm Sun, Feb 16, 2014

"You look fabulous!!! Do NOT change that hair!!!
A comment on a photo from today's event posted on Facebook.
If they only knew.

The Lithuanian Independence Day event was a success! It cost a lot more than I thought it would, but everybody was happy. We should make up the difference in donations.
We heard great ideas, the children sang and danced charmingly, people ate and enjoyed themselves.

My good friends staffed the registration table, took in the money, and dealt with the public.
I emceed and it worked out well enough. Mission accomplished.

One friend brought to the hotel where the event was taking place some mushrooms he'd picked and dried for me. Another brought me yellow and red peppers and green cabbage, the colors of the Lithuanian flag. Another neighbor had dropped off soup and cookies at my house in the afternoon, while I got to take home delicious celeriac soup from dinner tonight. Together with the lasagna that another friend had brought over last week, I am set. Love is shown in consumable ways...

Subject: Diana's Detour ~ 91
11:45 pm, Mon, Feb 17, 2014

Now that, according to the quiz on Facebook, the character on *Downton Abbey* I most resemble is the Dowager Countess Violet, allow me to bring up another one of my pet peeves: People who do not shovel their sidewalks when it snows.

Ours is a pedestrian-heavy neighborhood within a quarter mile of a metro station, so when residents don't clear off their sidewalks, that leaves a dangerous surface of bumpy shiny slippery crust to try to navigate. Some folks just cross the piles of snow plowed onto the curb and walk in the street.

All you have to do is take a broom and sweep early and often, and you can get rid of the snow while it's still fluffy and dry. Even when it gets deep, so long as you get to it quickly, it's relatively easy to remove. Then the sun helps melt it, and the path is clear.

However, if you don't, the sun melts the trampled surface, then it refreezes into an impassable mess. I noticed these lapses as I walked .9 miles to a meeting of the Silver Spring horticultural club tonight. There's a life lesson in here somewhere...

Subject: Diana's Detour ~ 92
10pm Tues, Feb 18, 2014

Three articles on cancer in today's Health and Science section in the Washington Post.
Can I be more of a textbook case?
    Median age at diagnosis of uterine cancer: 62
    Median age at death: 71 (that's a lot better than my current prognosis!)
The absolute worst, and most prevalent, is lung cancer.

My 50-ish neighbor, who is so sick with pancreatic and colon cancer, says they have now changed his diagnosis. It might be lung cancer. He's already had the whole "collarbone to navel" open surgery, but the cancer had spread too much to be picked out and hot chemo-washed. And this hit him just last May. He had gone to doctors with stomach issues a year before, but no one ever tested him for cancer because he "looked so healthy..."

But he clarified something for me. The reason they stop chemo after six months is that if it's going to work at all, it will have worked by then. The drill is scans every three months after that. If something appears, they try a different drug.

It must be different getting chemo to shrink a tumor that exists, as opposed having no tumor anymore and getting it to prevent cancer coming back. Mine is the latter, and it feels so much more hopeful.

Subject: Diana's Detour ~ 93
11:30 pm, Wed, Feb 19, 2014

I'm feeling the Neulasta shot, just a bit, throughout the bones in my body. That's a good sign. They're making blood cells!

My older brother sent me wristbands to help with seasickness and morning sickness and any other kind of queasiness one might feel. He had used them for a cruise in the Caribbean. I will be seeing all of my siblings this weekend, as well as my 90-year-old mother, in Cincinnati. Thanks for the sale, Delta.

Went to see "Symphony of the Soil" tonight after work. If it's not a gala, it's a composting film...

Subject: Diana's Detour ~ 94
11:15pm, Thur, Feb 20, 2014

Olympics. Ukraine. I have hardly mentioned them, but they have always been in the background.

I can't believe I have another 12 days before another chemo. I feel good, and that will be the final set.

The snow is starting to melt, but we're supposed to get at least one more snow. That's fine with me. It was a very beautiful fall, and this has been a real winter. I'm in no hurry.

Subject: Diana's Detour ~ 95
11pm Fri, Feb 21, 2014

The local guy who started a car service after his divorce asked me how I take my coffee.

He's picking me up at 4:30 am for a 6 am flight tomorrow morning.

He is also the one who took me to the hospital on a morning too icy for friends to risk their cars.

The mothers from our mother-daughter book club (Mothers Without Daughters now) met tonight, because we hadn't in so long.

Our daughters are all grown up, finished with college, and on to the next chapters in their lives, whether in California or Pittsburgh or Vietnam or staying right in the neighborhood.

Some have significant others. Others don't. There's no right recipe. No right age.

I've always liked the Russian proverb "Life is not just a walk across a field."

Subject: Diana's Detour ~ 96
Noon, Sat, Feb 22, 2014

No Wi-Fi, and senior citizen surrounded, I am "embedded" among the eighty and ninety-year olds and their canes and walkers in a gorgeous setting (French-door windowed corridors, skylights, beautiful masonry). Evergreen

Retirement Community in Cincinnati used to be a grand vineyard.

One of the women my mother and I lunched with yesterday (Mary Ann) turned out to be the mother of a friend of my sister's from Sacred Heart. Both registered nurses, Mary Ann has 5 daughters and Mary Beth is the mother of 6. Ah, the mothers who produced the baby boomer era...

They are in "assisted" living (not "independent" like my mother) and lament the lack of good conversation partners at meals. "Assisted" is where you go when you can't remember to take your pills on time, and wind up with "the demented" ... which they clearly were not.

What amazing things happened in Ukraine yesterday! And the Sochi Olympics are closing tonight. Have the stars aligned?

Subject: Diana's Detour ~ 97
10:30 pm Sun, Feb 23, 2014

Beautiful Olympics closing ceremony but, ahem, Mr. Putin, Marc Chagall (Siegel?), the pre-eminent Jewish artist of the 20[th]century, was actually born into a Lithuanian Jewish family in Liozna, near the city of Vitebsk, Belarus, which was part of the Russian empire in 1887 only the same way Lithuania was dominated. So no, that does not make him Russian. Although many bios say Chagall is Russian because it's easier not to sweat the details (where the devil is always lurking). But thank-you, Vladimir, for a spectacular display based on Chagall's art, especially the upside down villages. Loved it!

Cannot believe how inane the NBC commentators were when it came to describing what comprised the closing ceremonies! Would it have detracted from the ballet performances to know who composed that beautiful music? How about the impressive literary display? But in NBC's Vladimir Posner's words, "I'd tell you the names of the authors, but the list would be too long and boring." Really? Tolstoy, Dostoyevsky, and Solzhenitsyn they briefly mentioned. How about Pushkin, Gogol, Pasternak, etc.? And maybe some of their famous works? Is that really too much information for an American audience?

Will remain embedded among the elderly in Cincinnati through Monday. Made cabbage rolls for my mother today. She doesn't understand why I bother.

Subject: Re: Diana's Detour ~ 98
11:30 pm Mon, Feb 24, 2014

Back in DC. Kitty waiting for me.
As well as piles of mail, newspapers. But my bare-rooted red currants came in!

Snow tomorrow?
Mardi Gras in a week.
I'll be in chemo on Ash Wednesday.

The rituals are all about sweeping out, beating back winter and welcoming spring, being reborn.

I like the connection of Easter with estrus: The modern English term *Easter*, cognate with modern German *Ostern*, developed from the Old English word *Ēastre* or *Ēostre*. "This is generally held to have originally referred to the name of an Anglo-Saxon goddess, Ēostre, a form of the widely attested Indo-European dawn goddess. " How interesting that the word for dawn in Lithuanian, "Aušra," is pronounced oh-shra. That must make it politically correct to say "Happy Easter!"

Subject: Diana's Detour ~ 99
11:15 pm Tues, Feb 26, 2014

So tired after work today, I slept past my stop on the metro. But it was a power nap, all of about a minute long, and refreshed me.

Ankles swollen, but probably from standing while cooking and air travel over the weekend.
My toes are pretty much numb all the time now ~ neuropathy.
And the hair loss, my mother asks. Down there?
Really?
Well look at my arms, my legs, hardly any hair left there. Do the math.

The eyebrows are tricky as they get more sparse. Amazing how much we depend on them to frame our eyes.
I've still got my brows mostly, and enough of the other so that today, "snowflakes [do!] stay on my nose and eyelashes."
It was a snow globe kind of day.

Snow-flakes
By Henry Wadsworth Longfellow (1807–1882)[10]

Out of the bosom of the Air,
  Out of the cloud-folds of her garments shaken,
Over the woodlands brown and bare,
  Over the harvest-fields forsaken,
    Silent, and soft, and slow
    Descends the snow.

Even as our cloudy fancies take
  Suddenly shape in some divine expression,
Even as the troubled heart doth make
  In the white countenance confession,
    The troubled sky reveals
    The grief it feels.

This is the poem of the air,
  Slowly in silent syllables recorded;
This is the secret of despair,
  Long in its cloudy bosom hoarded,
    Now whispered and revealed
    To wood and field.

Subject: Diana's Detour ~ 100
10:45 pm Wed, Feb 26, 20141

It was an unexpected snow to wake up to this morning, and
that's always fun, if you like surprises, and I do.

Am I looking forward to my last chemo next week?
I guess so.
Have to talk to the radiologist on Friday.

Don't relish the port removal that will have to happen soon after.

I just don't like being cut.

The hysterectomy was so radical. I understood that recovery would take a while.

The port I would rather keep in forever, just in case.

Focus on Phoenix for early April....

Subject: Diana's Detour ~ 101
11:45 pm Thurs, Feb 27, 2014

"It's times like these you should rejoice that you daughter knows about make-up" wrote my own and sent me something called "Brow in a Box" by Urban Decay.... thanks also to my co-worker who recommended a henna product from Bigen. Eyebrows seem to be a problem for more than just cancer patients. Sometimes they are just too light to be noticeable. Other times too heavy and get plucked away too severely. It feels so old-fashioned to be painting them on. A Cambodian manicurist with perfect eyebrows once told me her secret — tattoo!

Thank you to everyone who reads these emails, comments, calls, texts, and sends me their prayers, love, and good wishes in so many ways. I have passed 100 days on this magical medical tour, which has been made so much more bearable because of you. Getting in shape with boot camp must have strengthened my body to handle the chemo, and a lifetime of friendships and work and community involvement buoyed my spirits.

The wind's picking up outside. Temps dropping to 12 tonight. Such a freezing February, but such warm hearts surround me.....

Subject: Diana's Detour ~ 102
11:20 pm Fri, Feb 28, 2014

Every time I am scheduled to have chemo, there is a snow event!
And so it looks like we're going to have snow again next week.

Today was the coldest day in February. Thank goodness that's over.

With the end of my chemo in sight, I spoke about "survivorship" with my oncologist today.
She strongly recommended some radiation.

Then I spoke with the radiologist.
The treatment would last 20 minutes each day for 5 weeks.
She assured me I could go to work normally, and the radiation would not hurt.

She also said it would not improve my overall survival rate.
So why would I do it?

It's a controversial treatment.
And she wants to do no harm.

We came to an impasse.
We'll meet again in about a month to discuss....

Subject: Diana's Detour ~ 103
11:45 pm, Sat, Mar 1, 2014

Russia has invaded Ukraine.
Another snowstorm is bearing down upon us.
My brother is due to fly in from Detroit this week for my last chemo.

Going down to demonstrate in support of Ukraine tomorrow.
I have always been nervous about how long the countries that were once under Soviet domination would get to hold onto their independence. Lithuania has been recognized as independent since 1991. That's only 23 years. But time for a whole generation to grow up thinking that's how it's always been.

Those of us who know better are nervous.

Subject: Diana's Detour ~ 104
11:45 pm, Sun, Mar 2, 2014

Walked 4 miles today between pro-Ukraine demonstrations at DuPont Circle and then at the Russian Embassy on Wisconsin Avenue.
Somebody said they saw me interviewed on the evening news.

Could barely stay awake through the Oscars.
Now waiting for the snow, 5-10 inches of it.

Everything is closed tomorrow: all metro buses, the government, my workplace, all schools.
It's good my chemo isn't scheduled until Tuesday.
Mardi Gras.

Subject: Diana's Detour ~ 105
11:15 pm, Mon, Mar 3, 2014

What a paralyzed day meteorologically, but what an exhausting day politically.
Drafting letters to congressmen and senators and the White House in support of Ukraine.
Trying to keep up C-SPAN and CNN and breaking news on all fronts.

A US foreign policy that started out sounding like "I couldn't care less" now seems to have some teeth.

My brother flew in from Detroit on schedule at 7pm.
Dug my car out for chemo tomorrow.

Subject: Diana's Detour ~ 106
11:15 pm Tue, Mar 4, 2014

"Can I have your autograph?" giggled a receptionist at the cancer infusion center today. Several people had seen me briefly on TV Sunday evening. But I had missed the 6 o'clock news, and the late night news had been overwhelmed by coverage of the snow and the Oscars.

At chemo, as soon as they give me the Benadryl, which is about 10 am, I am out like a light for hours.

But when I awoke about 1 pm today, there was my oncologist at the foot of my recliner, hands on her hips, tapping her foot, saying she'd spoken with the radiologist and with my nurse this morning about my reluctance to take the radiation.

She admitted there was no data to support what she wanted to do. "So I'm a guinea pig," I said. She is very good-hearted and laughed, and admitted yes. There's previous data (of which for my particular disease there is precious little) and then there's her gut instinct. Well, I appreciate the honesty.

Subject: Diana's Detour ~ 107
2:33 am, Thur, Mar 6, 2014

Doing so well after chemo, burgers and fries with my daughter's friend who picked me up, got some errands done in the afternoon thanks to coffee, and had a lovely dinner at home with a good friend.

But then fell asleep, forgot to take both sets of meds until way late.

Still red and puffy.
Won't be able to make the mass demonstration today at the White House at 1.

Tomorrow is my last day of chemo. But I have flowers for my nurse, and will get her a gift card to the in-house Au Bon Pain.

Au revoir it will be.

Subject: Re: Diana's Detour ~ 108
11:45 pm, Thur, Mar 6, 2014

Ugh. Just let me sleep.
I'll be fine tomorrow.
Perhaps there will be snow.

Subject: Re: Diana's Detour ~ 109
10pm, Fri, Mar 7, 2014

Bleh. Better, but still.
There's no trophy at the end of chemo.

Acupuncture. Neulasta shot.
Then had to get horizontal again.

Took a walk into my town.
Met a friend.
Came home and found my nephew and his wife had sent
me roses.
My trophy!

Subject: Diana's Detour ~ 110
10:45 pm Sat, Mar 8, 2014

> 7am morning coffee
> A little lie-down
> Picked up new eyeglasses at Stanley Kaplan's
> 10:30 am Photo op with Lithuanian Minister of
> Education in Rockville
> Meeting re Saturday school's financial situation
> Pick up wine and flowers at grocery store
> Home to grab some soup and send around some emails

3:30 pm Afternoon Mass at Shrine; got belated ashes on my hair instead of my forehead (that's apparently how they do it in the old country)
Traffic through Chevy Chase to Rockville
6:30 pm Art opening
7:30 pm Concert
Home again

Now I feel so much better.

Subject: Diana's Detour ~ 111
9 pm Sunday, March 9, 2014

There's nothing to beat the semi-queasies like a brisk walk in 50 degree weather with the snow finally melted, birds belting out in spring song, and sunshine pouring through bare-limbed trees. I saw wild crocus in bloom, the kind that carpet our lawns, and something tiny and yellow that I could not recognize (possibly Sagebrush buttercup (ranunculus glaberrimus) or Winter Aconite (eranthis Hyemalis)?) Plus, a very red-headed bird (not a cardinal; perhaps a woodpecker) was at my hanging suet cake this morning. A black squirrel dashes away noisily every time I pick up the seed tray that's fallen from atop my chimnea. Can it really have jumped onto it?

Too much time at the computer makes for more queasiness and less actually accomplished.
The body knows what is bad for it.
Movement and fresh air are good.
Email and Facebook are not.

Subject: Diana's Detour ~ 112
10:45 pm, Mon, March 10, 2014

So the woman who wrote "The Vagina Monologues," Eve Ensler, had uterine cancer, too. In "The Body of the World: a Memoir of Cancer and Connection," she connects her own illness to the devastation of the earth, her life force to the resilience of humanity, and her recovery to joining the body of the world.

My writer neighbor friend, showed up with a copy of the book after work today. I don't extrapolate my experience to the world beyond, but staying connected to the world is saving me. Cancer is what it is. Getting to be as common as chicken pox. It either kills you or it doesn't.

While visiting, my neighbor's husband picked up on my need to move some stuff to my attic in anticipation of houseguests arriving this evening.

I love Takoma.

Subject: Diana's Detour ~ 113
11:30 pm, Tues, Mar 11, 2014

So proud of my computer skills at work.
So happy to be able to ride the rails and read en route.
So glad to have a day warm enough to enjoy a fire in the chimnea outside in the evening.

Today was significant for those of us who pay attention to democracy rising and receding in the world.

On March 11, 1990, a pianist parliamentarian declared the restoration of Lithuanian independence.
Tonight, his daughter and her two sons are my houseguests after playing a piano/flute concert at the Embassy.

Post-concert pizza and wine outside.
Toasts at the picnic table with friends to a great performance.
But we are all concerned.

Subject: Diana's Detour ~ 114
9 pm Wed, Mar 12, 2014

So tired, going to bed early tonight.
I had awoken this morning bathed in a stinky, chemical sweat.
When I went to see my acupuncturist after work, she said she could smell the chemicals on me.

How can this be? My chemo ended almost a week ago.
She said it's cumulative.
So it's over, but not quite over yet.

Who is that man with the shiny bald pate stepping into a skirt and blouse and jacket?
Oh, it's me, sans wig.
A shock I will never get used to.
My body is still processing the chemical warfare. New hair will take a while.

Subject: Diana's Detour ~ 115
11:15 pm Thur, Mar 14, 2014

Between the wind and the cold and the flowers edging up through the soil, it's a real March.
March "was named for Mars, the Roman god of war."
The war is between winter and spring, trying to get winter to go out the door!
In Lithuanian, this month is called "Kovas," the word for battle.

My good friend gave me a ride home from work this evening.
This morning I was glad for the wig and the fur hat to keep me warm on the walk to the metro.

They're calling for flip-flops on Saturday but maybe snow on Monday.
I'm feeling better and love all weather.

January cold and desolate;
February dripping wet;
March wind ranges;
April changes;
Birds sing in tune
To flowers of May,
And sunny June
Brings longest day;
In scorched July
The storm-clouds fly,
Lightning-torn;
August bears corn,

September fruit;
In rough October
Earth must disrobe her;
Stars fall and shoot
In keen November;
And night is long
And cold is strong
In bleak December."

Christina Giorgina Rossetti, The Months, 1830-1894
1893 "Sing-Song"[11]

Subject: Diana's Detour ~ 116
9 pm, Fri, Mar 14, 2014

Even though I'm not an academic, there's a conference I had
really wanted to go to this weekend at Yale.
I would have seen a lot of old friends and been re-inspired
in my nonprofit outside-of-work work.
But guilt overtook me.

- I didn't feel right asking for two days off the week
  after my last chemo (during which my salary was
  always paid).
- I knew my boss was working on a project and
  counted on my help.
- I will be taking off for a week in Arizona soon.

I rationalized that I could use the rest.
But as soon as I take it easy, I start to feel queasy.

Subject: Diana's Detour ~ 117
11:15 pm, Sat, Mar 15, 2014

Yes, I played in the dirt today. Couldn't help myself.
It was sunny and warm, and there will be snow for St.
Patrick's Day.

Sent to me from a neighbor....

A Year of Being Here
daily mindfulness poetry by wordsmiths of the here & now
In this 03/15/2014 edition:

Barbara Crooker: "March"[12]

*Walking in the woods, thinking about the coming war,
late snow sifting down, I startled some geese
in the nearby cornfields; they took off in squadrons, bugles
blaring; the whump, whump of their wingbeats, rotors
in the wind. I was thinking about Li Po's "Grief in Early
       Spring,"
and I grew colder, knowing what lies ahead, all those sons
flying off with bright fanfares, returning home in silence.
Here, the Jordan Creek cuts through the marshes, rushing
over stones, over pieces of ice. And the snow keeps on falling,
softly, lightly—the coverlet a mother might settle on a cradle,
as she watches her newborn sleep to make sure he's breathing,
his small chest still moving, up, and down.*

Subject: Diana's Detour ~ 118
11:45 pm, Sun, Mar 16, 2014

About 3 inches of snow outside, and still coming down beautifully.

A few of us walked the mile to and from AFI (American Film Institute) in Silver Spring to see "Following the Ninth," a film about Beethoven's Ninth Symphony filmed in China, Chile, Japan, and Germany. It's considered Beethoven's hymn to human connection across all borders.

"And since June 29, 1985, Ode to Joy has been recognized by the European Union heads of State and governments as the **European anthem***, representing the community that has brought peace and freedom to its member countries."...is one of the symbols that celebrate their mutual values as well as their unity in diversity." (Wikipedia)*

http://www.youtube.com/watch?v=I90_deaEFus

Tell me I didn't hear this same tune on the news tonight with fireworks and Russian flags accompanying the "vote" in Ukraine's Crimea to "join" Russia...

Subject: Diana's Detour ~ 119
10:00 pm Mon, Mar 17, 2014

Trying to find an article I saw on Facebook that bemoaned the fact that the most literary and poetic and singing nation in the world, Ireland, is reduced now to green beer, leprechauns, and shamrocks.

Was surprised to read that there are only 5 million people in Ireland. And I thought Lithuanians made a lot of noise for their 3 millions strong size...

For the record, there are almost 6 million people in Maryland. I don't think we make that much noise.

Feeling so good, I just can't help, every once in a while, googling my disease and being shocked to be reminded of the prognosis. Will be getting scanned next week, and then every three months after that, whether I get radiation or not.

I'm visualizing a complete cure.

Subject: Diana's Detour ~ 120
11:00 pm Tues, Mar 18, 2014

I must be very conservative.
There's a video circulating on FB about the tremendous love that a group of women showed their friend who got cancer by shaving their heads in a show of solidarity.

I would be so embarrassed.
I would worry about the peer pressure that went into such a gesture.
I would be uncomfortable about the attention that it drew.

Then again, I'm older.
I remember films showing scores of shaven headed victims in concentration camps.
Of other women who'd had their heads shaved for fraternizing with the enemy.

I hide rather than flaunt my bald head.

Because I find it kind of scary looking.
I also find it cold, and there's still snow outside!

So here's to those of us who are shy and hide.
If that makes me a coward, so be it.
I'll take "I like your new hairstyle" as an affirmation.

And if my friends all want to run out and buy wigs, I won't
be embarrassed.

Ode to the shy.....

A Minor Poet[13]

I am a shell. From me you shall not hear
The splendid tramplings of insistent drums,
The orbed gold of the viol's voice that comes,
Heavy with radiance, languorous and clear.
Yet, if you hold me close against the ear,
A dim, far whisper rises clamorously,
The thunderous beat and passion of the sea,
The slow surge of the tides that drown the mere.

Others with subtle hands may pluck the strings,
Making even Love in music audible,
And earth one glory. I am but a shell
That moves, not of itself, and moving sings;
Leaving a fragrance, faint as wine new-shed,
A tremulous murmur from great days long dead.

Stephen Vincent Benét (1898-1943)

Subject: Re: Diana's Detour ~ 121
11:30 pm Wed, Mar 19, 2014

One hundred and twenty-one days after chemo began, and thirteen days after it ended, I am still losing eyelashes.
I guess I have not yet rounded the corner so far as bodily changes are concerned.
Otherwise, feeling fine, working, living normally.

The snow has almost melted, even though we may get some more next week.

"The future is today" says the main attorney I work for, who in the past two weeks has managed to put on the market and sell their family home in Potomac, buy a townhouse in Georgetown, get his taxes done, plus keep churning out the work.

He's right. The time to do anything is now.

Meanwhile, history is repeating itself in ways we hoped it never would.

Subject: Diana's Detour ~ 122
10:00 pm Thur Mar 20, 2014

The problem with a CT scan at 9 am is that you have to start drinking the berry barium at 7am.
Which means I have to get up at 5 and leave at 6 to be there by 7. (Later, I will figure out that I can drink the first dose of barium at home if I remember to get a bottle).
So that's what I'll be doing bright and early Friday morning.

Plus getting blood work.

Plus having an appointment with the oncologist who wants me to do radiation therapy.
Perhaps it's time to switch oncologists.
I like her very much. She's very perky and enthusiastic.
But she wants to throw the kitchen sink at me because she thinks I can take it.

Subject: Diana's Detour ~ 123
9pm Friday, Mar 21, 2014

I'm cured!
At least, my scan is clear!
And my red blood count is above 10, and my oncologist says she's never seen blood counts go up at the end of chemotherapy.

And she motioned to zip her lips and throw away the key about radiation therapy.
She says it works in all the rhabdo cases she's seen (in children) but if I don't want it....
Some people want everything thrown at their cancer.
Others are choosier.
And consider quality of life.

With radiation, "they never tell you about the scar tissue" said the tech administering the CT scan.
"You're going to be white on top and black on the bottom," said my next-door neighbor, Arnetta.

"My main concern is that it weakens your pelvic bones in producing bone marrow and blood cells," admitted my oncologist.
You could end up having diarrhea for the rest of your life.
Plus, it may promote other cancers...

"So when does it come back?" I asked.
"Do you really want to know?" she responded.

The statistics are skewed to look awful, because with my cancer there are too few cases and hence little funding to run studies, and the data out there include everyone who doesn't get any treatment at all. So having a 35% chance of making it 5 years sounds awful, but you can't rely on that information because there's so little of it, and it includes too much variation.

If I were a planner, I would have a two-year plan and a five-year plan.
But I'm not much of a planner except in case of a crisis, or with houseguests coming over....

Next scan in three months. Keeping my port in, just in case, although it has to be flushed every month to prevent blood clots.
And now that she's not pushing radiation, I'm beginning to think about it. But not going there yet....

There's a great video clip on FB about people in Klaipeda dancing to Pharell Williams' "Happy."
With developments in Ukraine, we're all feeling vulnerable, especially the Baltic countries, but also those who believe in

the rule of law and the value of democracy, and see it being rolled back…
Perhaps history will show that, for a brief twenty years of time, there was a reason to be happy.
http://tv.lrytas.lt/?id=13953922551393500891

Subject: Diana's Detour ~ Let's make it 124 & 125
9:30 pm Sun, Mar 23, 2014

This is for Saturday and Sunday.
I missed writing for my detour for the first time!
My excuse is that my daughter came home for Spring Break, we were up until 1 am, and I slept until 10 am on Sunday, which I never do.

Am I done? I don't know.
I don't want to think about it.

Today, my daughter made me watch a few episodes of "What not to wear."
Then we emptied my closets and threw things away and bagged a lot for donations.

I had done something similar with my friend a few months ago.
It just goes to show how much I still need to get rid of.

Decades of clothes.
Garments I should have given away in the last millennium.

Then we went shopping, just for me, as my daughter has given up shopping (for herself) for Lent.

I had dropped two dress sizes before getting cancer, by attending bootcamp almost every morning for $1^{1/2}$ years at 5:30 am.
I was in the best shape of my life.
It was a decision I'd made after turning 60.
I wanted to keep the blood flowing and to be strong in my later years.
And I did get strong, and flexible, and lost some weight, and did things I never thought I would be able to.

That's when cancer hit.
On vacation. At the beach. Over last Labor Day weekend.

I have actually had two people claim that I got cancer because I must have stressed my body out with too much exercise.
I prefer what my niece wrote to me: "I figure I better keep bootcamp-ing it so I can be strong enough to punch cancer in the face like you one day if I have to! :)"

Subject: Diana's Detour ~ 126
11 pm Mon, Mar 24, 2014

My daughter tells me I have to stop referring to her and her generation as "young people."
I didn't realize I do this. She says it's not necessary, and makes me sound old.
Wow.

Embarrassed that what I thought was a new-apartment-warming for one of those young people turned out to be an intimate "glad you've survived cancer" celebration for me! Thank you so much.

I am taking tomorrow off to spend some time with my daughter (she flew in from CA to spend spring break with me).

Plus, there's a 5 pm candlelight vigil at the Victims of Communism memorial and a book presentation at the Embassy "Children of Siberia," and the translator is my houseguest. I just wish the weather were a little less like Siberia. We are expecting an inch or two of snow, and it's almost April.

Could it be that Putin's incursion into Ukraine is actually a blessing in disguise, a wake-up call to the world that, hey, you can't think that aggression is over just because it quiets down for a while, like for 20 years.... like cancer.

Subject: Diana's Detour ~ 127
11 pm, Tues, Mar 25, 2014

It snowed so beautifully all day,
Covering the grass but not the streets or sidewalks.
Enough to dazzle but not paralyze.

Because I work, I don't often get to enjoy the low sunlight that moves throughout my rooms on winter days .
It's low on the horizon, and there are no leaves to filter out the sun.

And when snow covers the ground, there's an extra bonus of reflected brightness.

A day taken off from work seems like such a rich vacation to me.

My daughter here for her Spring Break.
Arizona next week.
California in mid-June to see my son.
Cincinnati before then to see my mother…

I need to get my port flushed this week.
I haven't had it removed.
Not yet.

Subject: Diana's Detour ~ 128
11:30 pm Wed, Mar 26, 2014

Going to the dentist for my semi-annual visit tomorrow.
So much has happened in the last six months.
Since my last check-up, I've been diagnosed with cancer, had a hysterectomy, and gone through six rounds of chemotherapy.
Happily, apart from the scar on my belly and a body temporarily devoid of hair, I am none the worse for wear.

I just wish it weren't so cold….a body needs its fur.

Subject: Re: Diana's Detour ~ 129
10:00 pm Thur, Mar 27, 2014

My dental hygienist is considering getting a pre-emptive radical mastectomy because her sister had breast cancer. She'll check first to make sure she is genetically predisposed herself. At age 55, she wants to protect herself.

My local friend with a tremendously difficult cancer story (that started only last May) has been hospitalized three times since the new year, and most recently contracted a hospital-borne pneumonia with "acute delirium." Plus he keeps suffering intestinal blockages.

No wonder I feel so fortunate.

Subject: Diana's Detour ~ 130
10:30 pm, Fri, Mar 28, 2014

It actually got into the 60s today!
I felt like a bear coming out of hibernation.

My daughter said no thanks to a flute concert at the Latvian Embassy (what a wealth of free events there are in Washington, DC) but asked to meet up with her and her friends afterwards at Kramer Books at Dupont Circle, if I knew where that is.

Yes, I know where that is. I used to work at that bookstore (30 years ago), in the evenings, after my fulltime job at the NAS, to "meet people" (ha!). Not so much fun as you might think it would be. I actually foiled a book robbery there, and got scolded by management for trying to be a hero. And the cafe and the book sides barely tolerated each other. Still the case, I understand.

And yes, I can find my way to the car at 17th & S. These were my stomping grounds once upon a time (1978-80), when I lived at 1630 Corcoran Street, my first apartment in DC, with the claw foot bathtub, bay windows, tall ceilings, and fireplace. Also, orange shag rug, rats outside in the daytime, and a noisy 5am delivery by semi every morning right under those bay windows to the McDonald's 30 feet away across the street.

So to see my daughter and her friends hanging out where I used to hang out reminds me how long I've been around, and how life goes on beyond you, in a good way.

Subject: Diana's Detour ~ 131
Sat, 11:30 pm, Mar 29, 2014

A friend stopped by in the rain to drop off a beautiful handbook about Phoenix, Scottsdale and Sedona this afternoon.

It turns out that the Biltmore Arizona, where the destination wedding is to take place, is in "1,000 Places to See Before You Die" by Patricia Schultz and known as "the Jewel of the Desert."
My friend in Sedona has booked us a trip to the amazing Antelope Canyon, which is around #7 at the following link:

http://distractify.com/culture/32-surreal-places-that-actually-exist-on-earth-i-cant-believe-this-isnt-photoshopped/

It is hard to imagine I will be enjoying these earthly wonders in just a few days.
Would I have planned this trip if I hadn't feared it would be one of my last?
Have I turned into one of those cancer survivors with a "bucket list?"
If so, is that so bad?...

Subject: Diana's Detour ~ 132
11:45 pm Sun, Mar 30, 2014

No one expected winter to come roaring back,
especially not the folks who waited until about 1pm today to finally call off the annual DC Kite Festival.

But snow it did, after the non-stop rain that later turned thick, then icy, and finally into sloppy flakes.

"So much weather!" my daughter sighed as she boarded a morning flight back to California.
But in California, there's never a chance of a snow day.
And some of us like surprises.

I Have a Rendezvous With Life[14]

I have a rendezvous with Life,
In days I hope will come,

Ere youth has sped, and strength of mind,
Ere voices sweet grow dumb.
I have a rendezvous with Life,
When Spring's first heralds hum.
Sure some would cry it's better far
To crown their days with sleep
Than face the road, the wind and rain,
To heed the calling deep.
Though wet nor blow nor space I fear,
Yet fear I deeply, too,
Lest Death should meet and claim me ere
I keep Life's rendezvous.

Countee Cullen (1903-1946)

Subject: Diana's Detour ~ 133
11:45 pm Mon, Mar 31, 2014

My mantra should be, I'm never fully prepared, but things always seem to work out for me.
I am sure I will forget to pack something for this trip to Arizona tomorrow.

A friend from college and I will meet after I pick up my car to stroll in the Phoenix Desert Botanical Garden and see the Chihuly glass sculptures installed there.
Then my friend from Sedona and I will rendezvous at Montezuma's castle for a hike.

Not bad planning for a first day. They are flexible for me, and I really appreciate it.

But now that I'm not under any active treatment, having said no to the radiation, I am constantly worrying about whether my cancer is coming back. Perhaps it's human nature to always want to do something, anything, even if it's the wrong thing, just to be doing something. Sitting back and waiting for nature to take its course, one way or the other, seems unproductive.

Perhaps I'll find a healing vortex in Sedona.

Subject: Diana's Detour ~ 134
10pm Tues, Apr 1 2014

Greetings from God's country! The air is fresh and dry, the sky is blue and clear, the ocotillo and agave are in bloom. I see what I think are Fireflowers showing off their red blossoms along the highway, hardy and happy only in tough circumstances, like our blue chicory back home.

"Vat a country!" And what a different beauty is the desert. National forests are seemingly endless hills dotted with low-growing bush that, once you ascend 4,000 feet then dip into the Green Valley, make way for giant red buttes. With the setting sun upon them, they are majestic.

Tomorrow we hike and explore vortexes.

Subject: Diana's Detour 135
11:45 pm Wed, Apr 2, 2014

"Bedazzled" — that's what people call my friend who moved to Sedona from Washington, DC, and she still turns heads when she walks into a crowd. Sports a jewel-studded black leather jacket, turquoise and feather bedecked cowboy hat, and boots, and, of course, she drives a Mercedes with one pocketbook dog and another Cockapoo that she's gotten designated a service dog, just because. Says she felt the onset of healing powers after waking up from a kidney operation with the doctors saying, "We almost lost you." She believes she can help heal me. We all need a friend like that.

Subject: Diana's Detour 136
11:45 pm Thur, Apr 3, 2014

We actually saw a sign at Big John's Texas Barbecue in Page, AZ, that read "We reserve the right to refuse service to anyone." I thought even the governor of Arizona, Jan Brewer, had vetoed that, realizing it might look bad for Arizona to be reintroducing Jim Crow laws, this time aimed against gay people. And here it was hanging in a restaurant. We turned around and walked out, and found a wonderful Mexican Fiesta restaurant down the street, with pictures of Laura Bush on its walls.

I remember my friend in Phoenix muttering, "We don't talk about Texas in Arizona."

Our foray through the corkscrew walls of Antelope Canyon, a narrow winding slit open to a sky peeking through swirly red rock formations, was as fantastic as the pictures had led us to believe. Among crowds of camera-phoned tourists and professional photographers with their tripods, the Navajo guides managed to corral us through passages open to the sky that were often barely wide enough to fit one person, and still allowed us to get "awesome" (in the true sense of the word) pictures. And no, "126 Hours" with James Franco was not filmed here, but one could look up and easily imagine him getting stuck in one of those openings.

At one point, my friend suddenly wrapped her arms around me from behind and quietly performed a brief healing ritual right then and there. She said she had felt a power. We turned a corner and our guide mentioned that we had just passed through one of the strongest healing points in the canyon.

"Bedazzled" is an astronomy buff in addition to being the author of "The Technology of God," so our day ended at Lowell Observatory in Flagstaff, observing Jupiter and four of its moons through a telescope, and enjoying celestial beauty from a low-lit spot on earth.

What astounding creation surrounds us.

Subject: Diana's Detour 137
11:10 pm, Fri, Apr 4, 2014

I have left the heavenly land of teal hillsides and terra cotta colossuses.
Traveling south, the mountains grow darker in color, and up pop saguaro cactuses along Route 17, with their up-stretched arms, eerily human-like.
And then the palm trees, signaling arrival in Phoenix.
Summer reportedly starts here tomorrow.

Someone on FB posted this today:

The thought manifests as the word;
The word manifests as the deed;
The deed develops into habit;
And habit hardens into character;
So watch the thought and its ways with care,
And let it spring from love
Born out of concern for all beings…
As the shadow follows the body,
As we think, so we become.

Buddha, Dhammapada (rephrased)[15]

Subject: Re: Diana's Detour 138
8pm Saturday, Apr 5, 2014

Checked into the Arizona Biltmore on Friday night, where my daughter was already lounging by the pool.
All wedding guests were taken (in three buses!) to a peak called "A Different Point of View" for wine and pre-wedding socializing.

The Biltmore is the kind of elegant place where my law firm would hold a partner retreat. Historic luxury à la Frank Lloyd Wright.
A massive campus of hotels and villas, planted in geraniums, pansies, and snapdragons, set against the backdrop of Camelback Mountain.
The fire pit seemed scented with cumin.

The wedding was not to be held until 6 pm so we had time to explore and enjoy elegant poolside living.

However, my daughter says I do not do luxury well. Not interested in massages or facials or the spa, we found a place in a nearby mall to get $12 manicures.

In any event, something happened, whether it was food poisoning from the breakfast that had left both of us feeling a bit queasy, or a bad reaction to a Tequila Sunrise cocktail at the pool, hopefully nothing worse, but I wound up bailing on the wedding. I could not even make it through the reading of the vows in the beautifully landscaped courtyard. Sick as a dog in my room, experiencing projectile vomiting such as that not seen since "The Exorcist," contorted with lower-back pain in a pillow-top bed, I tried all night just to sleep away the ache.

This is so not me, and it was so sad to be here in Arizona and not be able to attend the wedding of the son of friends of mine from graduate school in Bloomington. But my daughter kept checking on me by text, as she gamely represented our family by herself at the celebration.

Subject: Diana's Detour 139 & 140
11pm Mon, Apr 7, 2014

This is for Sunday and Monday, which I could not have survived without my college friend in Phoenix who took me in and let me sleep at her house until my red-eye back to DC at 11:30 pm (why I had to take the red-eye is a story of ineptitude on my part).

I got to work by 10am because my new flight took me to Washington National Airport, but the whole day I felt like

I'd just come back from chemo. It was evaluation day, plus it never looks good to take a sick day after vacation. I guess it was a perfect storm of food poisoning, radical altitude changes, riding around in a bumpy jeep over desert sands, and the long hours of driving that had affected my back, or just running around a lot, that led my body to rebel. Perhaps I'm not at 100% yet after all.

But I'll take tomorrow off and try to go to my oncologist, who said to call her if ever there was anything different. What's different is feeling like I still am in chemo. I thought I'd shaken that off for good. It's been over a month since my last treatment.

Subject: Diana's Detour 141
11:45 pm Tues, Apr 3, 2014

Took it easy, slept, then did some yard work because it felt so good to be out in the sun when it was 60 degrees, and slept again.

My daffodils were battered by the rain on Monday, but they've recovered now.
You can never have too many daffodils.

I know, I know, Wordsworth composed this poem totally from notes his sister Dorothy had made after a walk they both took. But it is still lovely.

I wandered lonely as a cloud[16]

I wandered lonely as a cloud
That floats on high o'er vales and hills,
When all at once I saw a crowd,
A host, of golden daffodils;
Beside the lake, beneath the trees,
Fluttering and dancing in the breeze.

Continuous as the stars that shine
And twinkle on the milky way,
They stretched in never-ending line
Along the margin of a bay:
Ten thousand saw I at a glance,
Tossing their heads in sprightly dance.

The waves beside them danced; but they
Out-did the sparkling waves in glee:
A poet could not but be gay,
In such a jocund company:
I gazed—and gazed—but little thought
What wealth the show to me had brought:

For oft, when on my couch I lie
In vacant or in pensive mood,
They flash upon that inward eye
Which is the bliss of solitude;
And then my heart with pleasure fills,
And dances with the daffodils.

William Wordsworth (1770-1850) 1804

Subject: Diana's Detour 142
Wed April 9, 2014 11:45 pm

Tomorrow is the birthday of my beloved late sister-in-law Britt, who loved flowers and gardens and everything that grew, especially her children. So sad that she didn't get to see her first grandchild, who will be turning one year old very soon.

To think that she was felled by aneurysms at age 50.

I miss her still.

Some lives don't have to be long to be very full....

From my eulogy to her:

Britt was non-judgmental by nature, a quality I particularly appreciated at the time that I met her, when I was a teenager. She accepted us all, said she looked forward to being our sister-in-law, and seemed actually interested in us as individuals.

But I grew to learn that that was her way. She didn't crave attention, but gave it. She didn't complain, but fixed. She didn't criticize, but contributed.

I got to visit Britt when she was a young bride in Athens, Ohio, and a young mother in Gainesville, Florida. It couldn't have been easy to be a graduate student's wife and a Danish woman in these small American towns. But Britt always managed to bloom where she was planted. Her focus was her home and her family. These values may not have been held in very high esteem in the seventies and eighties, but she stuck by them, and now when I look at Anton and Nina, I see why.

Britt put down roots in Oak Park, Illinois, and when it came time to move to Ann Arbor, Michigan, she did what needed to be done. Yards bloomed under her hands. Rooms came alive with her particular knack for combining the contemporary with the antique. Meals were a feast for palate and eye.

I will always treasure the fact that those of us who loved her so much got to spend Britt's last joyous days together with her that fateful Thanksgiving weekend in Cincinnati and Bright, Indiana. There was nothing special about it, but it was memorable in its simplicity. The food was good. The weather was gorgeous. And we were all together. Nothing, yet everything. The everlasting beauty of the everyday.

They say that the number of people in the world is always growing, but the number of good people remains the same. With the loss of Britt, the world has lost one of those truly good people, and we are all the poorer for it.

Another daffodil classic:

TO DAFFODILS[17]

Fair Daffodils, we weep to see
You haste away so soon;
As yet the early-rising sun
Has not attain'd his noon.
Stay, stay,
Until the hasting day
Has run
But to the even-song;
And, having pray'd together, we
Will go with you along.

We have short time to stay, as you,
We have as short a spring;
As quick a growth to meet decay,
As you, or anything.

We die
As your hours do, and dry
Away,
Like to the summer's rain;
Or as the pearls of morning's dew,
Ne'er to be found again.

Robert Herrick (1591–1674)

Subject: Diana's Detour 143
11:30 pm Thur, Apr 10, 2014

It's sprouting!
Turns out my scalp felt scratchy and uneven for a reason.
As of today, there's about a quarter inch of stiff spiky stuff growing on it.
Still losing eyelashes, but gaining hair cover... yay!

Good friends took me to the Kennedy Center again
And again I wonder why I don't go more often.
Heard a world renowned violinist, Gil Shahal, play a Stradivarius from 1699.
The piece was by Korngold, and his performance was magical.

It is magic, or perhaps metaphysical, what musicians create on stage.
And sitting very close, as we did, you feel present at the creation.

Beauty and music — an answer to life's inequalities.

Subject: Diana's Detour 144 & 145
10:30 pm Sat, Apr 12, 2014

I'm sorry, I don't seem to have anything interesting to say tonight.
Other than the weather is glorious,
We didn't get the storm and overcast skies that had been forecast for today
Just another beautiful warm spring day,
So even more people can enjoy the cherry blossoms.

Three events today: Lithuanian School at Embassy, Lithuanian Mass at Shrine, Folk acoustic band at Takoma VFW.
And lunch with a friend at DuPont Circle.
Still managed to sneak in a few hours of playing in the dirt, weeding.
It's a primal urge.

I am finally eyebrow and eyelash free, even as the hair on my head has begun to grow.
So odd.

Subject: Diana's Detour 146
1:45 pm Sun, Apr 13, 2014

Palm Sunday. 83 degrees.
2014 marks the 300th anniversary of the birth of a Lithuanian Lutheran pastor and poet, Kristijonas Donelaitis.
He wrote an epic poem, "Metai," about the toils of the peasants throughout the seasons.

Then I found this:

Prairie Spring
Willa Cather (1873-1947)[18]

Evening and the flat land,
Rich and sombre and always silent;
The miles of fresh-plowed soil,
Heavy and black, full of strength and harshness;
The growing wheat, the growing weeds,
The toiling horses, the tired men;
The long empty roads,
Sullen fires of sunset, fading,
The eternal, unresponsive sky.
Against all this, Youth,
Flaming like the wild roses,
Singing like the larks over the plowed fields,
Flashing like a star out of the twilight;
Youth with its insupportable sweetness,
Its fierce necessity,
Its sharp desire,
Singing and singing,
Out of the lips of silence,
Out of the earthy dusk.

Subject: Re: Diana's Detour 147
9:45 pm, Mon, Apr 14, 2014

Spring also brings out the crazies, unfortunately.
A 73-year-old anti-Semitic, white supremacist, KKK member opens fire at a Jewish community center in Kansas City at the start of Passover and kills three people - all of them white and none of them Jewish.

Should not have said, "Spring brings out the crazies."
That is insulting to people with mental health issues.
Hatred is an expression of free will.
How tragic that Spring and a religious celebration would elicit cold-blooded murder.

Subject: Re: Diana's Detour 148
11:30 pm, Tues, Apr 15, 2014

Taxes done and e-filed.
Am I the only one who prepares her own taxes any more?
I'm afraid I'll start owing the Feds once I can't claim my daughter as a dependent anymore.
Every year, my refund gets smaller and smaller.

I heard there was snow on the ground this morning in Cincinnati and in Chicago.
Flurries reported in Takoma this evening.
The heat is turned back on.

Someone asked what color is the hair that has sprouted on my head?
Very light so far.
What if it grows back grey?
How depressing.

Still tasting the chemicals. Last weekend's bout in Arizona with whatever it was set me back a bit.
Or my body is still trying to rid itself of the poisons that remained.

I wonder how my beautiful hyacinths will survive tonight's freeze?

Many had already flopped over, soaked in their waxy-bloomed weight.

It's just not fair for winter to be trying to make a comeback. We are all greened up and halfway through Spring.

Subject: Diana's Detour 149
9:30 pm Wed Apr 16 2014

So. cold.

The tulips and daffodils stood strong, but my hyacinths are history.

The water in the birdbath was frozen solid.

It's good Easter is so late this year; otherwise we'd be really confused.

Enjoyed a wonderful conversation last night with my friend who had had breast cancer five years ago and is now clear! She said radiation had been a snap after surgery and chemo, but her chest region doesn't harbor all those other bodily functions that might be affected. One always lives with the idea that it can come back, she says, but the idea of dying from cancer never crossed her mind.

She also said how much it would have helped her to be working throughout treatment. I can attest to that! Otherwise, you spend too much time with yourself, and she says she felt like a prisoner in her home, even with husband and grown children around her.

Normalcy is what you crave when you're faced with a situation that could knock you out of the real world. At least that's what I craved. Just get me back on the road I know.

Perhaps I'm not imaginative or brave enough to drop everything and go see all those places you're supposed to see before you die. I like where I am, and the life that I have, and to be able to still be a participant brings me great joy.

Subject: Diana's Detour 150
11:30 pm Thurs, Apr 17, 2014

Not at all tired tonight, but have a 9am flight tomorrow morning to Cincinnati for Easter.

Easter[19]

The air is like a butterfly
With frail blue wings.
The happy earth looks at the sky
And sings.

Joyce Kilmer (1886-1918)

Subject: Diana's Detour 151, 152, 153
11pm Sun, Apr 20, 2014

It's tough living in a place without Wi-Fi for three days. I have to take my computer to the Bistro area here at my mother's retirement community in Cincinnati to get any kind of Internet signal.

The Easter eggs have been colored and my niece's boyfriend wound up with the super egg that trounced everyone else's when we cracked with each other, on both the skinny and fat ends. We could not find beeswax for the batik-ing at the last minute, but at an old hardware store in Bright, Indiana, the solution came in the form of a $1.89 toilet bowl gasket, made of beeswax. Who knew?

My yeast bread braid was tasty if not pretty, and the birch log with the prune chocolate filling got done and decorated with pansies. Our breakfast served as hors d'oeuvres for the lamb dinner. We went to 9 am Mass at Xavier University where they mentioned my father among the parishioners who had died in the past year.

It's warm here, and stays lighter longer than in Washington. That's because Cincinnati is in the same time zone as DC, but 500 miles west.

Have to catch a 7 am flight tomorrow back to DC. Time to go to bed. Getting lots of input from folks who insist that my hair will come in curly; and I will miss the bald look....

Subject: Diana's Detour 154
10pm Mon Apr 21, 2014

Coming back into my life routine this morning, I can't believe I didn't mention a very important development over the weekend.

I had expected but did not get to see my one-year old grand-nephew because his Daddy had been admitted into a hospital for observation for something we hope will develop into nothing. In any event, it cast a pall over the entire Easter weekend. And although his Daddy was home after just one night, and we hope and pray that additional tests will prove him to be in the clear, it is still a reminder of how precious and precarious life is.

We are family top-heavy in the age department. Four siblings, all of us around sixty. My mother going strong at 90. Seven grandchildren in their twenties and thirties, but only one of them married ~ the Daddy mentioned above. And one great grandchild, almost one-year old.

Of course, we hope that, eventually, that one-year old will have maybe a brother or sister, and perhaps my own two children may provide him some cousins. But I didn't have kids until my late thirties, so if my children wait that long, will I ever see grandchildren, even if I outrun my cancer?

9 am Mass on Easter Sunday is like being in an Easter basket full of babies. It's nice to see. Like hearing a child babbling on a metro car full of adults ~ a pleasant reminder that life continues to be created, and to grow around me.

Subject: Re: Diana's Detour 155
10pm Tues, April 22, 2014

I love it when Google in its whimsy denotes a special anniversary by a play on the Google icon.

In honor of Earth Day today, Google's doodle was an homage to the Rufous hummingbird.

When we lived in San Diego for two years, our white plastic outdoor furniture was always dotted with poppy-seed-sized hummingbird droppings. So annoying. But here, I do

everything possible to attract them, and a sighting is as rare
a pleasure as the rainbow that appeared in today's 7 pm sky.

Ode to the Hummingbird by Pablo Neruda
Translated by George Schade[20]

The hummingbird
in flight
is a water-spark,
an incandescent drip
of American
fire,
the jungle's
flaming resume,
a heavenly,
precise
rainbow:
the hummingbird is
an arc,
a golden
thread,
a green
bonfire!
Oh
tiny
living
lightning,
when
you hover
in the air,
you are
a body of pollen,
a feather
or hot coal,

I ask you:
What is your substance?
Perhaps during the blind age
of the Deluge,
within fertility's
mud,
when the rose
crystallized
in an anthracite fist,
and metals matriculated
each one in
a secret gallery
perhaps then
from a wounded reptile
some fragment rolled,
a golden atom,
the last cosmic scale,
a drop of terrestrial fire
took flight,
suspending your splendor,
your iridescent,
swift sapphire.
You doze
on a nut,
fit into a diminutive blossom;
you are an arrow,
a pattern,
a coat-of-arms,
honey's vibrato, pollen's ray;
you are so stouthearted—
the falcon
with his black plumage
does not daunt you:

you pirouette,
a light within the light,
air within the air.
Wrapped in your wings,
you penetrate the sheath
of a quivering flower,
not fearing
that her nuptial honey
may take off your head!
From scarlet to dusty gold,
to yellow flames,
to the rare
ashen emerald,
to the orange and black velvet
of our girdle gilded by sunflowers,
to the sketch
like
amber thorns,
your Epiphany,
little supreme being,
you are a miracle,
shimmering
from torrid California
to Patagonia's whistling,
bitter wind.
You are a sun-seed,
plumed
fire,
a miniature
flag
in flight,
a petal of silenced nations,
a syllable

of buried blood,
a feather
of an ancient heart,
submerged

Subject: Diana's Detour 156
9pm Wed, Apr 23, 2014 8pm

I know my friends hate it when I say this, but if this were to be my last year on earth, the seasons have been pretty spectacular.

It was a glorious and long-lasting autumn. We had a very wintry winter. And now spring is taking its own sweet time unfurling its beauties and keeping them cool enough not to bolt.

Or cold, I should say. It's been a cold, cold spring, but the flowers seem to love it, so who am I to complain.

The Daddy of the one-year old does have what we feared, Guillain-Barré syndrome, but five days of hospital treatment should cure him, and for that we are very grateful.

Life is so intense when you are in your thirties, going full speed in your career, creating your family, establishing a home for them.

I observe from the sidelines, now, in awe and appreciation of their efforts, because they do bear fruit while they tire you out.

And somehow, all you want to do is get back in the mix.

All I want is for him to be healthy again.

Subject: Diana's Detour 157
11:30 pm Thur, Apr 24, 2014

The giant elm tree in my yard almost bit the dust a few years
ago, but resurrected unexpectedly.
I found what I wrote about it at the time.
It's leafing out beautifully again this year.

Ode to the elm
Long live the elm.

The elm, planted around 1966,
Now 10 feet around
Must have sensed its doom.
Pummeling the porch
With tree-sized branches
In Winter, and then again in Spring.
Barely bothering to leaf out anymore,
Stingy with its shade
Hovering menacingly.
Its roots upheaved my wooden fence
And split my neighbor's concrete drive
He hates that tree.
A deer impaled itself in the V
That ensued between post and gate.
And died quietly.
"No, it's a healthy American Elm
Dutch is just the name of a disease."
"Stegophora ulmea" more likely.
But by this April, not a sign of life.
Six companies came by to inspect
And give estimates for its removal.

Might as well take down the decapitated
Red cedar, too, bare in its midriff
Scraggly everywhere else.
A double amputation.
The red brick house will seem naked.
Green blankets removed from its shoulders.
And then, and then,
"Wait" said the arborist on the pending application.
"I think I saw something."
And he did. The azaleas over,
Long after all the other trees had sprung back to life,
The Elm decided to, too.
Leafing out with a vengeance.
Of course, I don't want to take it down
If I don't have to.
The birds are so much enjoying it
Its limbs lush with leaves.
The red cedar gets a reprieve, too.
Prune and elevate.
That's what I'll do come January.
Get it high off our houses.
Perhaps lop off some dangerous overhangs.
That'll cost as much as a tree removal.
They are that huge and heavy.
We live in terminal danger, my neighbors and I.
We've seen the havoc these limbs can wreak.
Yes, they do fall where we just stood.
The elm should never have been planted there,
Between our two houses. That's a fact.
My neighbor hates that tree.
Its roots do buckle and strain,
They slash through my grass.

And pulverize his driveway, mercilessly.
But where did it find water in this time of drought?
What possessed it to reclaim its lease on life
While we so cautiously plotted its decease?

Diana Vidutis
May 8, 2012

Subject: Diana's Detour 158
Friday, 8pm, Apr 25, 2014

Twenty-five years ago, I gave birth to a precious little boy who was so good-natured and easy that we decided to have another child within the next two years. I remain amazed by the whole experience.

Of course, becoming a mom changes your life entirely.
There is nothing more humbling or exalting.

On the one hand, you get to live life over again.
On the other hand, you are no longer you, but somebody's Mommy.

It's an experience of love so intense and overwhelming that it's hard to imagine you will ever be able to part from that child.
That's why God created teenager-hood.
It's part of nature's plan to help you both detach from each other.

What's the most shocking is that your children are not "mini-me-s."
I don't know what I was expecting, but the characters I created wound up being very different from me.
And that's not a bad thing.
In fact, it's a pretty interesting thing.
And I am forever grateful that they make me feel "au courant" with what young people (my apologies for over-using that term) are thinking these days.

My only regret is that, once launched, both of my children decided to live a continent away, in San Francisco.
As Garrison Keillor would say, **Be well, do good work, and keep in touch.**®

Subject: Diana's Detour 159
10pm Sat, Apr 26, 2014

Early morning coffee, then to the Franciscan Monastery for the annual plant sale.
What could be more fun?
Today was the first truly warm Spring day.
I finally got to take all my seedlings out from the basement and into the sun.
And the earth is still moist enough to make weeding easy.

So many weeds to pull, so much young growth to uncover from autumn's leftover leaves.
I've got ferns unfurling, and Solomon's Seal making its truly unusual early appearance.
The daffodils are spent; but the tulips are in full glory and azaleas ready to pop.

The lily of the valley are poking through.
It's always fun to see where the Virginia Bluebells decide to show up this year.
So truly delicate and ephemeral, floppy yet shyly showy.

The Bluebell
Anne Bronte (1820-1849)[21]

A fine and subtle spirit dwells
In every little flower,
Each one its own sweet feeling breathes
With more or less of power.

There is a silent eloquence
In every wild bluebell
That fills my softened heart with bliss
That words could never tell.

O, that lone flower recalled to me
My happy childhood's hours
When bluebells seemed like fairy gifts
A prize among the flowers,

160, 161, 162
10:30 pm Tues, Apr 29, 2014

Sense of impending doom.
I know it has to do with the weather.
Tornadoes moving in from the Midwest, where they've already taken 21 lives.
I'm just worried about my giant elm, and its limbs crashing down upon us.
Everything blooms beautifully under a dark cloud.

The best lighting for photos.
The color rich and saturated.
Surely, I'm just imagining things.

Then it hit this afternoon.
Six people fired from their jobs at my workplace.
I could never work in Human Resources and have to do that
to people.
And this evening, found out one of my favorite people has
a lung tumor.

Yes, I've just spent a lovely evening at the embassy rubbing
shoulders with Senators and Congressmen and sharing
stories of our days working there when Lithuania had just
becoming independent.
But you come home in the cold rain and turn on the heat in
the house.
And realize this day has not been a good one for many
people.

Subject: Diana's Detour 163
8pm Wed Apr 30, 2014

As long as this exists...

*"As long as this exists," I thought, "and I may live to see it, this
sunshine, the cloudless skies, while this lasts, I cannot be
unhappy." The best remedy for those who are afraid, lonely or
unhappy is to go outside, somewhere where they can be quite alone
with the heavens, nature, and God. Because only then does one feel
that all is as it should be and that God wishes to see people happy,
amidst the simple beauty of nature. As long as this exists, and it
certainly always will, I know that then there will always be*

comfort for every sorrow, whatever the circumstances may be. And I firmly believe that nature brings solace in all troubles. "As long as this exists..."

Anne Frank (1929-1945)
Excerpt from The Diary of a Young Girl. [22]

Subject: Diana's Detour 164, 165
Fri, May 2, 2014

I should go see the movie *Noah*.
We have emerged into a new world of warmth and sunshine since the deluge.

I am still scattering energy in many directions.
Feeling a bit adrift, not having to go to treatments on a regular basis,
responsible only to myself for getting my port flushed every 4-6 weeks
no more blood tests or scans for 3 months
I've fallen off from seeing my acupuncturist since before Arizona.
Now it's just a waiting game.

New idea is to be an observer in Ukraine for the elections May 25.
If I can find $2K to cover the expenses
And I can get time off from work (which I don't have).

If anything bad is going on inside, I won't know until after a scan in mid-June
After I've been to see my kids in California.
After lots more events and meetings

After much lawn mowing, weeding, gardening
Summer, at least the planting and the initial growing part,
will be basically over by mid June
When summer is officially just beginning.
You've got to plan so much ahead.

I can't believe Scandinavian Airlines actually gave me
partial credit for the ticket I could not use last October
When I'd planned to go to Lithuania for 2 weeks, and
wound up having a hysterectomy instead.
The new plan is to meet up with my daughter and her
boyfriend in Lithuania for the last two weeks of August this
year.
What a difference a half year can make...

Subject: Diana's Detour 166
10pm Sat, Mar 3, 2014

Got yelled at in emails by a couple of friends who said I was
crazy to consider being an election monitor in Ukraine just
after getting over cancer. Then again, who better to go into
a dangerous environment than someone with a death threat
hanging over her head?

Not focusing on that right now.
It's my grandnephew's first birthday.
He's already had three haircuts.
My own little boy was bald as a billiard ball for his entire
first year.

My home and yard were crying for attention today.
So I cut my Saturday events down from three to one.

And mowed my lawn instead.
Plus it's pure joy to play in the dirt when it's sunny and
warm outside and wild wisteria perfumes the air.

My Summer in a Garden[23]

The love of dirt is among the earliest of passions, as it is the
    latest.
Mud-pies gratify one of our first and best instincts.
So long as we are dirty, we are pure.

Fondness for the ground comes back to a man after he has run
    the round of pleasure and business,
eaten dirt, and sown wild oats, drifted about the world, and
    taken the wind of all its moods.

The love of digging in the ground (or of looking on while he pays
    another to dig)
is as sure to come back to him, as he is sure, at last, to go under
    the ground, and stay there."

Charles Dudley Warner (1829-1900)
My Summer in a Garden, 1870

Subject: Diana's Detour 167
11pm Sun, May 4, 2014

When we lived in San Diego for two years, people didn't
seem to do yard work the way we do around here.

They hired gardeners, installed irrigation systems, and left for the beach or the mountains on the weekends.
And it didn't rain very much.

Here, there is so much water to manage.
I live downhill from a huge neighborhood that drains into my yard.
Two sump pumps saved my basement during the recent deluge.
But one neighborhood yard I visited was an absolute bog.

The Takoma house and garden tour today was, as usual, inspiring and exhausting.
It was a nice break from my own weeding and planting.
And though my house and my yard are a fraction of their size, I have more than enough to keep me busy.

Like weeding my uneven lawn. I won't put down sod but keep weeding and seeding and feeding organically.

"When I have the time to take a walk, I would often take the time to admire the grass. Grass doesn't make a fuss. It doesn't try to be beautiful or outstanding. It doesn't want to attract attention. It is so humble that it even allows people to walk all over it. Yet, it possesses such strength. It glows in healthy green despite being stepped all over, and when a typhoon strikes and all the flowers die and all the trees get uprooted, humble grass survives. And humble grass, in its own humble way, provides food for animals, shelter for insects, and joy to some funny guy walking past. I think a virtuous man should be like grass. Humble, unnoticed, yet possessing great strength and kindness."

- Tan Chade Meng, the "Jolly Good Fellow" at Google[24]

Subject: Diana's Detour 168
11:30 pm, Mon, May 5, 2014

HR is OK with my going to Ukraine, and I got one phone call of support.

But I read somewhere that there were too many observers at the Ukrainian election last time.

Plus, I have no experience.

Plus, you can't express any opinions, and I think I would want to agitate, and that would not be allowed.

Like the time I went for facilitator training, and realized I just don't have the non-partisan personality required.

More good words about grass by the woman who wrote the song "Little boxes on the hillside."

Sings the truth - Malvina Reynolds - (1966)[25]

God bless the grass that grows thru the crack.
They roll the concrete over it to try and keep it back.
The concrete gets tired of what it has to do,
It breaks and it buckles and the grass grows thru,
And God bless the grass.

God bless the truth that fights toward the sun,
They roll the lies over it and think that it is done.
It moves through the ground and reaches for the air,
And after a while it is growing everywhere,
And God bless the grass.

God bless the grass that grows through cement.
It's green and it's tender and it's easily bent.

But after a while it lifts up its head,
For the grass is living and the stone is dead,
And God bless the grass.

God bless the grass that's gentle and low,
Its roots they are deep and its will is to grow.
And God bless the truth, the friend of the poor,
And the wild grass growing at the poor man's door,

And God bless the grass.

Subject: Diana's Detour 169 & 170
Wednesday, May 7, 2014

"I missed you guys!" I said upon entering the infusion center.
And it was the truth.
I had to go in to get some heparin flushed into the port still living beneath my collarbone.

I do miss my nurse and my doctor from the chemotherapy experience.
We went through a war together, and I think I got out alive.
In the five weeks since my last flush, two floors of the new hospital at Sibley have been constructed, and the reception office for infusion has moved.
I'm like an alumna going back to school and noticing how much things have changed.

And driving to the hospital was a delight in the riot of Spring color enveloping all the streets of Washington at this time of year.

The redbud, the magnolia, the wisteria .... beauty is balm to the soul.

Subject: Diana's Detour 171
Thursday, 10:00 pm May 8, 2014

Carpe Diem from 400 years ago.....

To the Virgins to Make Much of Time[26]
by Robert Herrick

Gather ye rose-buds while ye may,
Old Time is still a-flying:
And this same flower that smiles today,
Tomorrow will be dying.

The glorious lamp of heaven, the Sun,
The higher he's a-getting
The sooner will his race be run,
And nearer he's to setting.

That age is best which is the first,
When youth and blood are warmer;
But being spent, the worse, and worst
Times, still succeed the former.

Then be not coy, but use your time;
And while ye may, go marry:
For having lost but once your prime,
You may for ever tarry.

Subject: Diana's Detour 172
Fri, 10pm, May 9, 2014

One friend responded to yesterday's "To the Virgins to Make Much of Time" ...

"Aaargh! Actually, this was never such good advice for the Virgins - more like: here's an idea, you'll be sorry if you don't satisfy the young men in their lust (but let's not talk about the real consequences)."

But that's why these 17th century poets were called "the Cavalier Poets." Instead of tackling issues like religion, philosophy, and the arts, their poems praised both pleasure and virtue, mostly celebrating beauty, love, nature, sensuality, drinking, good fellowship, honor, and social life.

Another carpe diem ("Seize the Day") poem from 400 years ago, suggested by another friend, whose husband used it in courting her.

Who ever classified these as metaphysical?....

TO HIS COY MISTRESS[27]
by Andrew Marvell (1621–1678)

Had we but world enough and time,
This coyness, lady, were no crime.
We would sit down, and think which way
To walk, and pass our long love's day.
Thou by the Indian Ganges' side
Shouldst rubies find; I by the tide
Of Humber would complain. I would

Love you ten years before the flood,
And you should, if you please, refuse
Till the conversion of the Jews.
My vegetable love should grow
Vaster than empires and more slow;
An hundred years should go to praise
Thine eyes, and on thy forehead gaze;
Two hundred to adore each breast,
But thirty thousand to the rest;
An age at least to every part,
And the last age should show your heart.
For, lady, you deserve this state,
Nor would I love at lower rate.

But at my back I always hear
Time's wingèd chariot hurrying near;
And yonder all before us lie
Deserts of vast eternity.
Thy beauty shall no more be found;
Nor, in thy marble vault, shall sound
My echoing song; then worms shall try
That long-preserved virginity,
And your quaint honour turn to dust,
And into ashes all my lust;
The grave's a fine and private place,
But none, I think, do there embrace.

Now therefore, while the youthful hue
Sits on thy skin like morning dew,
And while thy willing soul transpires
At every pore with instant fires,
Now let us sport us while we may,
And now, like amorous birds of prey,
Rather at once our time devour
Than languish in his slow-chapped power.

Let us roll all our strength and all
Our sweetness up into one ball,
And tear our pleasures with rough strife
Thorough the iron gates of life:
Thus, though we cannot make our sun
Stand still, yet we will make him run.

Subject: Re: Diana's Detour 173
11:30 pm Sat, May 10, 2014

Ten thousand flowers in spring, the moon in autumn, a cool
*   breeze in summer,*
snow in winter.
If your mind isn't clouded by unnecessary things, this is the best
*   season of*
your life.

   —Wu Men (Japanese Zen master and poet) (1183–1260)[28]

Subject: Diana's Detour 174
Sunday, 10:15pm, May 11, 2014

May all Mothers have been told today that they were loved
and cherished.

When You Are Old[29]
William Butler Yeats (1865-1939)

When you are old and grey and full of sleep,
And nodding by the fire, take down this book,
And slowly read, and dream of the soft look
Your eyes had once, and of their shadows deep;

How many loved your moments of glad grace,
And loved your beauty with love false or true,
But one man loved the pilgrim soul in you,
And loved the sorrows of your changing face;

And bending down beside the glowing bars,
Murmur, a little sadly, how Love fled
And paced upon the mountains overhead
And hid his face amid a crowd of stars.

Subject: Diana's Detour 175
11pm, Mon, May 12, 2014

I must admit, I am suffering from iris envy.
So tall, so purple, rising majestic above sharp green leaves.
Making such a bold statement.
Spring is here. Now bring on the 90-degree weather.

For Mother's Day, my friend's foodie son grilled us a dinner
of grass-fed meat and all organic vegetables.
Given that my own two kids are far, far away, it was much
appreciated.
And her stands of iris are spectacular.

I love the outpouring of mother/daughter pictures on
Facebook to mark the occasion.
Realize that I am one of very few people my age to still have
a mother around.
And I am very lucky to be around for my own children.

Shockingly, the hair on my body is returning from the legs
on up.

Weirdly nothing on my arms.
And my head? Let's just say emergent short grey fur with some black markings.
The wig had added height to the crown of my head, which is sorely lacking in real life.
I'll no longer get the compliments I've been getting once I go back to my previous head shape and hairstyle...

Subject: Diana's Detour 176
9pm, Tues, May 13, 2014

Spring birdsong is so deafeningly beautiful to awake to these mornings.
Enough to make me turn off the NPR news that comes on my radio a little before 6am.
And just listen.

There is always plenty of bad news in the world.
The invasion of Ukraine. The kidnapped Nigerian girls. The collapsing Antarctic ice cap.

Little restores one's faith in the world so much as small creatures continuing with their natural business.

Subject: Diana's Detour 177
11:30 pm Wed, May 14, 2014

So I learned that in Britain, the term for early morning birdsong is "the Dawn Chorus."

*The **dawn chorus** occurs when songbirds sing at the start of a new day. In temperate countries this is most noticeable in spring when the birds are either defending a breeding territory or trying to attract a mate. In a given location, it is common for different species to do their dawn singing at different times. In a study of the Ecuadoran forest, it was determined that birds perching higher in the trees and birds with larger eyes tend to pipe up first. These correlations may be caused by the fact that both would also correlate with the amount of light perceived by the bird.*

Leave it to the Brits to even have an International Dawn Chorus Day
International Dawn Chorus Day is the worldwide celebration of Nature's daily Miracle.
http://en.wikipedia.org/wiki/Dawn_chorus_(birds)

Some thoughts on this.

Dawn Chorus[30]
By Sasha Dugdale (March 29, 2010)

Every morning since the time changed
I have woken to the dawn chorus
And even before it sounded, I dreamed of it
Loud, unbelievably loud, shameless, raucous
And once I rose and twitched the curtains apart
Expecting the birds to be pressing in fright
Against the pane like passengers
But the garden was empty and it was night
Not a slither of light at the horizon
Still the birds were bawling through the mists
Terrible, invisible

A million small evangelists
How they sing: as if each had pecked up a smoldering coal
Their throats singed and swollen with song
In dissonance as befits the dark world
Where only travelers and the sleepless belong

Subject: Diana's Detour 178
Thur, May 15, 2014

A friend's father died this week. He was 100 years old, from Venezuela, and devoted his life to tropical medicine, focusing on leprosy. Three thousand people came to his funeral in Caracas, including some 80 year olds whose leprosy had been arrested thanks to his efforts.

Growing up Catholic, we were always praying for those with leprosy and collecting dimes for them. Here was a man who tackled it directly. Who canonizes the saints of medicine?

Subject: Diana's Detour 179
Fri May 16, 2014

The extent of my procrastination is evident out my back windows and up the hill in my neighbor's back yard.
It is the annual march of the bamboo.
Every day that I don't go up and pull them down, they grow a foot taller.
Literally, hundreds of them. Every day. Some are now over 10 feet tall.

Not specifically in my yard, but they impact me once they get three stories tall and harden.
At this early stage, no matter how tall they are, they are still so soft you can kick them over and they collapse.
My neighbor is fine with my getting involved.
She doesn't see what I see. It's not her entire view, whereas, it is mine.

The hard part will be removing them rather than letting them lie where they collapse.
I will take down about 500 tomorrow, and hopefully make a dent.
It's an annual ritual.
I don't really hate it.
It's kind of a marvel actually.
Something between a phallic stomp and a rocket launch.

But in case anyone you know is ever tempted to throw up "quick-growing" hedge,
Just remember, friends don't let friends plant bamboo.

Subject: Re: Diana's Detour 180
Saturday, May 17, 2014

Ah, delicious exhaustion!
Spent hours taking down bamboo and cutting back wisteria, porcelain berry, winter creeper, English ivy, thumb ripper (aka Mile-A-Minute), multiflora rose, etc.
It's the only time I feel close to George W. Bush.
I understand the pleasure he reportedly took in cutting brush on his Texas ranch.

As it gets warmer, I may get close to ditching the wig.

Working outside and sweating means your head sweats.
Coming in to drink some water, I found I just couldn't put a wet wig back on.
So I used an earlier wig to finish.

It's good the weather has been so cold throughout all my bald days.
My wig has been good about keeping my head warm.
But now, well, we'll see.
I'm still not brave enough to go public with my small head and buzz of grey hair.

Subject: Diana's Detour 181
11:30 pm, Sun, May 18, 2014

Got a huge ostrich fern, a helleborus, and some naked lady (Amaryllis belladonna) bulbs at the Takoma Park Horticulture Club — A Hardy Perennial Since 1916 — plant exchange today.
My contribution was some Solomon's Seal and some Mexican primrose.
Sorted the bamboo I'd cut yesterday into useable lengths, but most of it is now at the end of my driveway to be picked up as yard waste tomorrow.

And then went to a First Communion.

All rites of Spring.

Subject: Diana's Detour 182
10pm, Mon, May 19, 2014

Got a request to gather my late father's archival materials and donate them to the Lithuanian Research and Studies Center in Chicago.
That will take some doing, but I was planning on visiting Cincinnati anyway the last weekend of this month.

It's what I feel least able to tackle. I think my father's papers are already pretty well organized and should be easy to go through, but I could never say the same about my own.

It would be really helpful if we all went through life and organized as if for an archive.

I know some people who are really good about it.
Saving only the one best piece of artwork from each year of each child's life.
I save too much, then can't find it. Or it all gets damaged when the basement floods.

Which is another way of saying I admire anyone who can self-document on a regular, organized basis.
A friend of mine once taught me to organize photos (back in the days of albums) not chronologically or by how they fit onto a page, but with a plot. Make the photos tell a story. Even give one a page of its own, if that will make it more interesting.

Then again, maybe the first thing one should do is to make sure that every photo is dated and the persons pictured identified.

I believe some more culling is in my future.

Subject: Re: Diana's Detour 183
10:00 pm Tues, May 20, 2014

I picked up the book at Carpe Librum, a "pop-up" used bookstore on 17th Street near Farragut Square.
By Katia Mann, widow of Thomas Mann, who had a house in Nida, Lithuania, a seaside resort called "Nidden" back in those Germanic days. My daughter Nida is named after this seaside town. And we have been to Thomas Mann's house, now a conference center.

Apart from "Buddenbrooks" (for which he won the Nobel Prize for literature) and "Magic Mountain," Thomas Mann wrote many other works.
And his wife writes about some of the real people he used as models for characters in his stories.
Like for something called "The Black Swan."

"I rarely gave him inspiration for his books" writes Katia Mann. "...I can only remember one conversation about a very late story, The Black Swan.".; not one of his major works, and many people don't like it. They find it unsavory. I, on the other hand, like it.....By the way, although I very seldom gave him ideas for his work, in this case I did inspire the story...."I once knew a woman, Frau So-and-so. She was in love with a younger man. One day she came triumphantly to tell me her secret: 'Just imagine! I've begun menstruating again." It turned out to be cancer of the uterus.'"

Too close for comfort....

Subject: Diana's Detour 184
11:00 pm Wed, May 21, 2014

Memorial Day Holiday weekend coming up, and I'm staying put, thank goodness.
It won't be warm enough to go swimming, but it's already warm enough to eat outside in the evenings, and that's always a delight.

Will my job give us early release on Friday? I hope so.
That way I can get a head start to go see Garrison Keillor at Wolf Trap that evening...

Subject: Diana's Detour 185
10:30 pm Thurs, May 22, 2014

My neighbor dragged me out to sit on the front porch this lovely evening.
Otherwise, I'm drafting emails while watching Midsomer Murders or Doc Martin.

She wants to know when I'm going to ditch the wig.
I understand hair grows about half an inch every month
Mine still hasn't made it to the first half inch.
It's going to be a long hot summer.

Subject: Diana's Detour 186, 187, 188
10pm, Sun, May 25, 2014

"Too bold?"
"No, Mom, too bald. You still look too bald."

That was the view from Palo Alto, my daughter's reaction to the head shot I had sent to her by cell phone.

She is also not a fan of the silver look.
"But with a lot of eye make-up, I could look like one of those ladies in the Chico's catalogue."

My daughter said she preferred the hair color I had before.

"Not even with a tan? And turquoise jewelry?"

"No."

I am lucky to have a beauty consultant, albeit on the West Coast.
My daughter must have gotten the glamour gene that my mother and sister both have, but skipped me, or I rebelled against it so much that it was beaten into recession.

I am also lucky to have friends who call when I don't post for a few days, concerned that I'm okay.
I am fine, but I tend to need more sleep than I used to.
Perhaps it's a delayed reaction to the chemo.
They said I would feel fatigue, which I never did, but maybe it's catching up with me now.
And then out of the blue, I'll feel a little nauseated. Weird.

It's been beautiful weather this Memorial Day weekend, and there's still one more day to go.
Lots of time to spend outside and dig in dirt.

But no sooner have I dug in the plants that I got at the plant exchange, than a friend loads me up with more interesting specimens.

It's always exciting to find something that grows well in shade, of which I have so much.

And then to try to solve the mystery of those spots where nothing seems to grow well ever.

I know, I know, ... amend, amend, amend the soil, and manage the water flow.

Subject: Diana's Detour 189, 190
10pm Tues, May 27, 2014

Have to hand it to those Estonians ~ providing DC with a free concert of music by the most performed living classical composer, Arvo Part, renting out the Concert Hall at the Kennedy Center, promoting it so it was filled to the rafters, and then presenting the composer at the end. Not bad for a country of 1.3 million, which also invented Skype. Also the target of a crippling cyber attack by Russia (142 million) back in 2007, not to speak of a 50-year long Soviet occupation after WWII. The Russian invasion of Ukraine was not a surprise to previous victims.

Memorial Day weekend reminds us how much we owe to those who come to our country's defense, and the defense of freedom around the world. And in whose hands guns should properly be.

Richard Martinez, father of one of the shooting victims at UC Santa Barbara over the weekend, stated: "I understand this is a complicated problem. I have friends who are in the NRA. I grew up on a farm. I hunted. I killed animals. I understand guns," Martinez said. "But assault rifles and semiautomatic weapons? There is no need for those except in war."

So my Memorial Day weekend was a quiet one of visiting friends, many friends, in between yard work and enjoying the beautiful outdoors locally ~ Wolf Trap, Bel Air, Takoma, Miller's Island, Forest Glen.

And I want to say Happy Birthday to Rachel Carson, whom Google honored with an online icon today. She lived here in Silver Spring, where she wrote "Silent Spring" in an effort to get us to avoid pesticides (specifically DDT) in our daily lives, in agriculture, and our local yard work. She would have been 107 years old.

Subject: Diana's Detour 191
9 pm, Wed, May 28, 2014

Washed over by summer rain.
A downpour overnight smashed down three levels of my tall and glorious pink Mexican primroses.
I had to beat off the rain in the morning,
the way we do with soggy snow that weighs down our bushes in winter,
so they have a chance of standing erect again.

Then it hailed in the middle of the day, around 3 pm, when no one was looking.
But I noticed, through the floor-to-ceiling glass walls of our offices on K Street.

Last night it was enchanting to emerge from the Kennedy Center at 8pm into streets drying from a cloudburst we must have missed.
Still light outside, the air so warm, you just wanted to keep on walking.

And it rains intermittently this evening.
I hear the swish of the cars on Piney Branch Road.
And the loud dripping on the leaves outside.

This time before air conditioners have to be turned on
When curtains still waft with the breeze.

Subject: Diana's Detour 192
11:00 pm Thu, May 29, 2014

STILL I RISE[31]
Maya Angelou, 1928-2014

You may write me down in history
With your bitter, twisted lies,
You may trod me in the very dirt
But still, like dust, I'll rise.
Does my sassiness upset you?
Why are you beset with gloom?
'Cause I walk like I've got oil wells
Pumping in my living room.
Just like moons and like suns,
With the certainty of tides,
Just like hopes springing high,
Still I'll rise.
Did you want to see me broken?

Bowed head and lowered eyes?
Shoulders falling down like teardrops,
Weakened by my soulful cries?
Does my haughtiness offend you?
Don't you take it awful hard
'Cause I laugh like I've got gold mines
Diggin' in my own backyard.
You may shoot me with your words,
You may cut me with your eyes,
You may kill me with your hatefulness,
But still, like air, I'll rise.
Does my sexiness upset you?
Does it come as a surprise
That I dance like I've got diamonds
At the meeting of my thighs?
Out of the huts of history's shame
I rise
Up from a past that's rooted in pain
I rise
I'm a black ocean, leaping and wide,
Welling and swelling I bear in the tide.
Leaving behind nights of terror and fear
I rise
Into a daybreak that's wondrously clear
I rise
Bringing the gifts that my ancestors gave,
I am the dream and the hope of the slave.
I rise
I rise
I rise.

Subject: Diana's Detour 193
10:30 pm Fri, May 30, 2014

Back in Cincinnati, in the land of walkers and canes, this evening my mother and I enjoyed the showing of a beautiful film, "The Book Thief."

This morning I learned that one of my friends in California has cancer, too.
I will get to see her when I visit my children in mid-June.
So glad we keep in touch.
So sad we have a bad visitor in common.

Soon it will be June.

The Months[32]
by Linda Pastan (b. 1932)

March
When the Earl King came
to steal away the child
in Goethe's poem, the father said
don't be afraid,
it's just the wind...
As if it weren't the wind
that blows away the tender
fragments of this world—
leftover leaves in the corners
of the garden, a Lenten Rose
that thought it safe
to bloom so early.

April
In the pastel blur
of the garden,
the cherry
and redbud
shake rain
from their delicate
shoulders, as petals
of pink
dogwood
wash down the ditches
in dreamlike
rivers of color.

May
Mayapple, daffodil,
hyacinth, lily,
and by the front
porch steps
every billowing
shade of purple
and lavender lilac,
my mother's favorite flower,
sweet breath drifting through
the open windows:
perfume of memory-conduit
of spring.

Subject: Diana's Detour 194
10:45 pm Sat, May 31, 2014

Whoever designed Evergreen in Cincinnati really knew what they were doing.

Would that all retirement communities, no, all public housing projects and all hospital grounds were designed this way!

From an aerial photograph, it looks densely laid out.

From the ground, however, the three-story buildings are charming, beautifully landscaped, walkways one leading into another.

French windows and daylight abound.

The elderly residents can walker its glass-paned corridors seemingly forever and see courtyards with bushes and flowers on either side.

Or if it's nice outside, they can walker outdoors to get to their apartments.

The healing power of nature is welcomed in.

The Want of Peace[33]
by Wendell Berry (b. 1934)

All goes back to the earth,
and so I do not desire
pride of excess or power,
but the contentments made
by men who have had little:
the fisherman's silence
receiving the river's grace,
the gardner's musing on rows.

I lack the peace of simple things.
I am never wholly in place.
I find no peace or grace.
We sell the world to buy fire,
our way lighted by burning men,
and that has bent my mind
and made me think of darkness
and wish for the dumb life of roots.

Subject: Diana's Detour 195
11:30 pm Sun, Jun 1, 2014

There's nothing like sorting through a father's papers and photos to make you realize you can't get it done in one weekend.

Fortunately, I understand Frontier Airlines has started cheap flights to Cincinnati from Washington Dulles. I'll have to check them out.

Life[34]
Edith Wharton (1862-1937)

Life, like a marble block, is given to all,
A blank, inchoate mass of years and days,
Whence one with ardent chisel swift essays
Some shape of strength or symmetry to call;
One shatters it in bits to mend a wall;
One in a craftier hand the chisel lays,
And one, to wake the mirth in Lesbia's gaze,
Carves it apace in toys fantastical.
But least is he who, with enchanted eyes

Filled with high visions of fair shapes to be,
Muses which god he shall immortalize
In the proud Parian's perpetuity,
Till twilight warns him from the punctual skies
That the night cometh wherein none shall see.

Subject: Diana's Detour 196
11:45 pm Mon, Jun 2, 2014

It's Mulberry season!
Noticed the blue splotches on the sidewalk as I was walking home from the metro today.
Looked up and picked some.
Seriously staining but delicious.

Mulberries remind me of my friend Tanya Heiberg from Indiana University.
A brilliant young pianist from Appleton, Wisconsin, she walked around in a perpetual state of wonder, and loved discovering mulberry trees on Bloomington's campus.

Tanya was such a talented musician; they allowed her, as a freshman, to study with Menahem Pressler of the Beaux Arts Trio.
She'd already studied with Andre Watts.
She was also very gifted in languages. We studied Russian together.

But Tanya dropped out of college her sophomore year to become a Moonie.
Because she wanted to save the world, right now.

She was seriously considering donating an eye to a blind person or finding someone who could use a kidney.
Instead, she joined the ranks of Rev. Sun Myung Moon.
In a mass 700-couple ceremony, she married someone the Unification Church had chosen for her.
And had two children.

She was pregnant with a third child, one she was carrying for another Moonie couple who couldn't conceive, when she was diagnosed with breast cancer.
That was 25 years ago. She refused treatment for herself in order to save the child.
After she died, her husband took her children somewhere to Australia, and her mother never saw her grandchildren again.

Mulberries always remind me of Tanya.
She was a gift to this world who was too good for this world.

Subject: Diana's Detour 197
10:30 pm Tue, June 3, 2014

Tomorrow marks some major world events:
June 4th, 1989, an extraordinary day. Tiananmen Square, Khomeini funeral - and the democratic elections that ended communism in Poland.
I was the mother of a six-week old son on this date in 1989, and we posed before the Lady Liberty statue in front of the Chinese Embassy.
Solidarność had finally triumphed in Poland. Lithuania would reestablish its independence nine months later.
Iran, well, that's another story.

Subject: Diana's Detour 198
11pm Wed, Jun 4, 2014

A June poem by the Hoosier poet James Whitcomb Riley, who also wrote:

> *"Little Orphant Annie's come to our house to stay*
> *An' wash the cups an' saucers up, an brush the crumbs away,*
> *An' shoe the chickens off the porch, an' dust the hearth an sweep,*
> *An' make the fire, an' bake the bread, an' earn her board-an'*
> *keep -"*

From James Whitcomb Riley's poem (1849-1916):
Knee-Deep In June[35]

VIII
March ain't never nothin' new!
Aprile's altogether too
Brash fer me! and May—I jes'
'Bominate its promises,
Little hints o' sunshine and
Green around the timber-land—
A few blossoms, and a few
Chip-birds, and a sprout er two,—
Drap asleep, and it turns in
'Fore daylight and SNOWS ag'in!—
But when JUNE comes—Clear my th'oat
With wild honey!—Rench my hair
In the dew! and hold my coat!
Whoop out loud! and th'ow my hat!—
June wants me, and I'm to spare!
Spread them shadders anywhere,
I'll git down and waller there,
And obleeged to you at that!

Subject: Diana's Detour 199
11:30 pm, Thur, Jun 5, 2014

Jacqueline Kennedy had asked the National Symphony Orchestra to play Samuel Barber's "Adagio for Strings" after her husband's funeral.
Paul Skevinton played it tonight on the organ at the Kennedy Center during a "postlude," a free after-concert concert.
My mother had asked for the same "Adagio for Strings" to be played at my father's funeral a year ago.
Mournful in a very inspiring way.

Subject: Re: Diana's Detour 200
11pm, Fri, June 6, 2014

Morning birdsong floats through my windows until the traffic picks up around 6am.
It's at its best 4-5 am... " I can't hear it enough said the tulip"

Song[36]
Alicia Suskin Ostriker

Some claim the origin of song
was a war cry
some say it was a rhyme
telling the farmers when to plant and reap
don't they know the first song was a lullaby
pulled from a mother's sleep
said the old woman
A significant

factor generating my delight in being
alive this springtime
is the birdsong
that like a sweeping mesh has captured me
like diamond rain I can't
hear it enough said the tulip
Lifetime after lifetime
we surged up the hill
I and my dear brothers
thirsty for blood
uttering
our beautiful songs
said the dog

Subject: Diana's Detour 201
11 pm Sat June 7, 2014

It was far too nice outside to spend the evening in a movie theater...

How often in Washington is it warm but not humid, with no bugs about?

A perfect night to grill hot dogs over coals, and heat beans in a cast iron skillet.

To enjoy hors d'oeuvres on the front porch, and watch passers go by.

The 20 foot bamboo poles in my driveway have attracted some takers.

It was the second harvest of this invasive tree.

Hardly any branches to trim off of these.

They really are beautiful.

I just wish I had a teepee or a lean-to to construct from them.

Subject: Diana's Detour 202
10:30 pm Sun, Jun 8, 2014

"I found a place to live, Mama. It's a group house, looks great, but someone got shot a couple of doors down a few years ago."
"So what? Don't you remember you're in the US now? That's normal there."

People think I'm generous for letting international visitors rent a room from me now and then.
They don't realize how much I learn from them, especially from the young ones.

Like my current millennial from Lithuania, who told me about the above conversation she had with her Mom when she first went to study documentary filmmaking in Missouri. Our gun-crazed culture is fascinating to the rest of the world, and not in a good way.

I may have written this before, but I think we should be honest about our priorities and hang a loaded gun on the wall of every classroom in the US, where Catholic schools would ordinarily have a crucifix and public schools a picture of George Washington. We should change our Pledge of Allegiance to read "One nation under Gun." This is what we have become.

Pay no attention to the fact that the recent shooter in Santa Barbara was stopped by pepper spray. What a concept.

And the mother who called the police for help with her suicidal son saw him shot to death by those same police. He flashed at them the knife he was going to use on himself, so they killed him.

Let me just go plant some more gladiolus bulbs.....

Subject: Diana's Detour 203
10:30 pm Mon, Jun 9, 2014

"This is June, the month of grass and leaves . . . already the aspens are trembling again, and a new summer is offered me. I feel a little fluttered in my thoughts, as if I might be too late. Each season is but an infinitesimal point. It no sooner comes than it is gone. It has no duration. It simply gives a tone and hue to my thought. Each annual phenomena is reminiscence and prompting. Our thoughts and sentiments answer to the revolution of the seasons, as two cog-wheels fit into each other. We are conversant with only one point of contact at a time, from which we receive a prompting and impulse and instantly pass to a new season or point of contact. A year is made up of a certain series and number of sensations and thoughts which have their language in nature. Now I am ice, now I am sorrel. Each experience reduces itself to a mood of the mind."

Henry David Thoreau (1817-1862)
Journal, June 6, 1857 [37]

Subject: Diana's Detour 204
Tues, Jun 10, 2014

"If you're going to San Francisco
Be sure to wear some flowers in your hair
If you're going to San Francisco
You're gonna meet some gentle people there

For those who come to San Francisco
Summertime will be a love-in there
In the streets of San Francisco
Gentle people with flowers in their hair

All across the nation such a strange vibration
People in motion
There's a whole generation with a new explanation
People in motion people in motion

For those who come to San Francisco
Be sure to wear some flowers in your hair
If you come to San Francisco
Summertime will be a love-in there"

—San Francisco (Be Sure to Wear Some Flowers in Your Hair). Written by John Phillips(sung by Scott McKenzie).[38]

Subject: Re: Diana's Detour 205
Wed Jun 11, 2014

I still get childish pleasure from taking off in a plane and seeing the toy-like world pull away as we zoom into the clouds, through the clouds, and then up into the big blue sky, leaving that soft, fluffy layer below us, like Heaven is supposed to be.

I was expecting to have Wi-Fi on this United flight from DC to San Francisco, but no such luck. Not only does this airplane not seem to be wired for Wi-Fi, it doesn't have any monitors at all, for movies or announcements. So much for in-flight entertainment. Is this a new development? If everyone is expected to bring along their own laptop or iPad, then there is no need for overhead or seat monitors anymore?

Yes, apparently it is. This is a new airplane, and United's CEO has stripped it of all amenities except for Wi-Fi, which, by the way, doesn't happen to be hooked up yet. "All Jeff-ed up" they say, as Jeff is the name of the CEO responsible for these changes. Worth a word to United.com.

I must admit, the de-cluttered look does have mid-1950s feel to it. And it is boon to those of us who like to read or look out the window, but that return flight in the dark is going to be a long one. I usually count on these cross-country trips to fill in my gaps in popular culture.

Subject: Diana's Detour 206
Thursday, June 12, 2014

Just as mulberries remind me of my pianist friend from Bloomington Tanya, and Marimekko fabrics remind me of my sister-in-law Britt, so does the miracle of compound interest remind me of my IU and DC friend Mary Lee, the third dearly departed member of my trifecta trinity.

I viewed one retirement account today to realize that it had earned $2,000 in the past 7 days. Unbelievable on the one hand, obscene on the other, as I realize I how I benefit from the mechanism that widens the income gap in this country.

And this just an accident of some good advice I took thirty years ago, part of it coming from Mary Lee. And Andrew Tobias' "The Only Investment Guide You'll Ever Need," and David Childton's "The Wealthy Barber." Small amounts of money put away early into high-risk investments and forgotten just keep on growing exponentially, even if the stock market plummets precipitously several times….The Miracle of Compound Interest.

Mary Lee, the most unlikely source for such wisdom. Legally bind, mastering Russian and Arabic by magnifying glass, she welcomed me into her basement efficiency at 7th and D Streets Southeast near Eastern Market when I first moved to Washington. We had studied Russian together at Indiana University, and for jobs in the late 1970s you went either to NY or DC. I had no business savvy back in those days of Détente, (nor do I now!) so I chose DC and the non-profit world of international exchanges.

Mary Lee morphed eventually from Russophile to IT expert at the National Academy of Sciences. "I read the manuals," she'd explain. "No one else wants to."

She was proud of being a Marfan, although that disease brought about her untimely death at 44 from a bisected aorta. Marfan syndrome, Abraham Lincoln's disease, in which your arms measured from fingertip to fingertip are longer than you are tall, characterized by slightly protruding eyes and ribcage, spatulate fingers, connective tissue issues, and eventually heart problems.

I lose count of how many people she accommodated in various alcoves of that basement apartment in 1978. Several of us remain friends to this day. I guess we're middle-aged now, even senior citizens, but you're always the same age to your friends. Before marriages, before kids, before careers. You stay to each other what you were, back when it counted.

Subject: Diana's Detour 207
Friday, June 13, 2014

It takes me a while to readjust to California.
I remember when I first saw it, with a delegation of Soviet scientists visiting wind turbines.
The overwhelming impression was brown.
This is a desert. But when you add water, it is miraculous.

The air is so very fresh here. No humidity.
And the fragrance of pepper trees and jasmine.

When we lived in San Diego for two years, I was concerned that Christmas would seem weird without snow.
Then I told the kids it would be much more like where Christ was actually born, in Bethlehem.

I loved today's post-dinner outing to a horse ranch.
Actually, a non-fancy place to board horses on the outskirts of Stanford University.
California the way it used to be ~ dusty, scrub brush, low hills, panoramic.

Subject: Diana's Detour 208
Sat, Jun 14, 2014

I saw a shooting star in the sky tonight,
Driving on I-280 from Palo Alto to San Francisco.
Please, let my scan be clear on Friday.
Otherwise, I will feel really guilty about not doing the radiation....

If I hear the word "passion" one more time at a commencement speech or any other life advice-giving event, I will give a silent scream, and recall August Rodin's massive sculpture "The Gates of Hell, which, by the way, I got to enjoy today at Stanford University's Art Museum.
"Their turbulent bodies form a discontinuous narrative centered on the theme of humanity's hopeless and painful enslavement by passion."

Whoa. I know we're talking about different "passions" here, but perhaps there is some connection. I guess people in the 19th century did not have to be told to be passionate. They were obsessed by it. Passion seethed and boiled, and was something that needed to be reined in. An eternity in hell was the punishment for it.

Reportedly, over the years, Rodin's "Doors" project evolved into something much less like hell and more like life. *"Instead, the figures on the doors poignantly and heart-renderingly evoke universal human emotions and experiences, such as forbidden love, punishment, and suffering, but they also suggest unapologetic sexuality, maternal love, and contemplation."*

We also know many of the figures as separate sculptures like "The Thinker," "The Kiss," and my favorite: "She Who Was Once the Helmet-Maker's Beautiful Wife (Celle qui fut la belle heaulmière) or The Old Courtesan.

Thank you, August Rodin, who never saw these gates cast in bronze while he was alive.

Rodin and I share a birthday, November 12th. We also share this birthday with Grace Kelly, Tanya Harding, and Charles Manson. People with a passion.

Subject: Re: Diana's Detour 210
Mon, Jun 16, 2014

Reading a book about George Soros in which he expounded considerably on the idea of death, describing it as "a private horror which every individual must deal with as best as he can."

One avenue, he said, was to ignore it, which was what "the large, faceless masses of society, who are not very much aware of their own individual existence, are doing."

Another was "to identify oneself with a larger unity which will survive the individual and through which one can transcend one's own finite experience."

That, "he continued, "is what those who have trained themselves to accept death as the inevitable sequel to life have done, including myself."

He seems quite the tortured soul in the book, a frustrated philosopher, wanting to do something significant, mainly to please his parents. Very much along the lines of, we are special, we are superior, but we are insecure enough to have to work obsessively to stay on top.

Subject: Re: Diana's Detour 211
11:30 pm, Tues, Jun 17, 2014

For those who might argue that if you like too many things,
you don't really value anything ....

Miracles[39]
By Walt Whitman (1819-1892)

Why, who makes much of a miracle?
As to me I know of nothing else but miracles,
Whether I walk the streets of Manhattan,
Or dart my sight over the roofs of houses toward the sky,
Or wade with naked feet along the beach just in the edge of the
    water,
Or stand under trees in the woods,
Or talk by day with any one I love, or sleep in the bed at night
with any one I love,
Or sit at table at dinner with the rest,
Or look at strangers opposite me riding in the car,
Or watch honey-bees busy around the hive of a summer
    forenoon,
Or animals feeding in the fields,
Or birds, or the wonderfulness of insects in the air,
Or the wonderfulness of the sundown, or of stars shining so
    quiet
and bright,
Or the exquisite delicate thin curve of the new moon in spring;
These with the rest, one and all, are to me miracles,
The whole referring, yet each distinct and in its place.

To me every hour of the light and dark is a miracle,
Every cubic inch of space is a miracle,
Every square yard of the surface of the earth is spread with the
    same,
Every foot of the interior swarms with the same.
To me the sea is a continual miracle,
The fishes that swim — the rocks — the motion of the waves — the
ships with men in them,
What stranger miracles are there?

Subject: Diana's Detour 212
Wednesday, June 18, 2014

Vacation[40]
Rita Dove (b. 1952)

I love the hour before takeoff,
that stretch of no time, no home
but the gray vinyl seats linked like
unfolding paper dolls. Soon we shall
be summoned to the gate, soon enough
and perforated stubs — but for now
I can look at these ragtag nuclear families
or the heeled bachelorette trying
to ignore a baby's wail and the baby's
exhausted mother waiting to be called up early
while the athlete, one monstrous hand
asleep on his duffel bag, listens,
perched like a seal trained for the plunge.
Even the lone executive
who has wandered this far into summer
with his lasered itinerary, briefcase

knocking his knees—even he
has worked for the pleasure of bearing
no more than a scrap of himself
into this hall. He'll dine out, she'll sleep late,
they'll let the sun burn them happy all morning
—a little hope, a little whimsy
before the loudspeaker blurts
and we leap up to become
Flight 828, now boarding at Gate 17.

Subject: Diana's Detour 213
Thur, June 19, 2014

Hot town, summer in the city
Back of my neck getting dirty and gritty
Been down, isn't it a pity
Doesn't seem to be a shadow in the city

All around, people looking half dead
Walking on the sidewalk, hotter than a match head

But at night it's a different world
Go out and find a girl
Come-on come-on and dance all night
Despite the heat it'll be alright

And babe, don't you know it's a pity
That the days can't be like the nights
In the summer, in the city
In the summer, in the city

Cool town, evening in the city
Dressing so fine and looking so pretty
Cool cat, looking for a kitty
Gonna look in every corner of the city

Till I'm wheezing like a bus stop
Running up the stairs, gonna meet you on the rooftop

But at night it's a different world
Go out and find a girl
Come-on come-on and dance all night
Despite the heat it'll be alright

And babe, don't you know it's a pity
That the days can't be like the nights
In the summer, in the city
In the summer, in the city

"Summer in the City"[41] was a 1966 hit single by The Lovin'
Spoonful, written by Mark Sebastian (brother of John
Sebastian) and Steve Boone. It came from their album,
Hums of the Lovin' Spoonful. It reached number one on the
Billboard Hot 100 on August 13. The song featured a series
of car horns, during the instrumental bridge, starting with a
Volkswagen Beetle horn, and ending up with a jackhammer
sound, in order to give the impressions of the sounds of the
summer in the city. The song is ranked #393 on the Rolling
Stone magazine's list of The 500 Greatest Songs of All Time

Subject: Diana's Detour 214
1:30 pm Fri, Jun 20, 2014

Scan is clear!
My first scan three months after completing chemotherapy came back clear!

This is much better news than I had expected.
I was beginning to feel "movement" in my pelvic area, like cells multiplying.
I was beginning to think I should have gone for the radiation after all.
How utterly irresponsible of me not to have done that.
I was sure my oncologist would come in today and say "Told you so!"

But none of that happened. My CT scan shows no new developments.
Thank God/goodness for no news, because it really is good news!

"When did your symptoms start?" she asked. "A week or two ago?"
"Yes."
She chuckled.
"A case of 'scan-itis.' I see it all the time. A week or two before a scan, the patient starts feeling new aches and pains and suspicious activity. It's very typical."

So good to hear it was all in my head.

"Do you want to get your port out?"
"I don't know."

"Do you want me to make a command decision for you?"
"Yes!" said my friend who had accompanied me to the appointment. "I mean I wouldn't know what to do, and I would want someone in the know to make that decision for me."

On this, I had to agree.
This wonderful oncologist is the one who recommended a much more debilitating form of chemotherapy, and was outvoted.
She is also the one who was really pushing radiation as a supplement to the surgery and chemotherapy, and I know I really worried her when I opted not to.

But on removing the port, I think I'm fine with that.
Next Tuesday? OK, although that's pretty quick. But my workplace will prefer I take off a Tuesday rather than another Friday.

I cannot believe we are actually rounding a bend.

My oncologist says I have to come back for scans every three months for the first two years.
Once we get to the two year mark, we can breathe more easily, and it will be twice a year for the three years after that.

I am breathing much more easily already!
My oncologist says she has seen cancer come back in some patients by the first scan.
This means it hasn't. And every clean scan under one's belt is one step closer to that two-year mark.

Yes!

Subject: Diana's Detour 215
Saturday, June 21, 2014

Vernal Sentiment[42]
Theodore Roethke (1908-1963)

Though the crocuses poke up their heads in the usual places,
The frog scum appear on the pond with the same froth of green,
And boys moon at girls with last year's fatuous faces,
I never am bored, however familiar the scene.
When from under the barn the cat brings a similar litter,—
Two yellow and black, and one that looks in between,—
Though it all happened before, I cannot grow bitter:
I rejoice in the spring, as though no spring ever had been.

Subject: Diana's Detour 216
Sunday, June 22, 2014

A day cool enough for the windows to be left open and the AC left off.

Went to 9am Mass (hedging my bets).
Had my car washed and cleaned inside and out.
Picked up a native Monarda at the Farmer's Market, bee almost included.
Picked up some petunias, hipoestes, manure, and leafgro at the hardware store.
Also a rudbeckia (Black-eyed Susan, Maryland's native flower),
As mine seem to have been eaten by deer.
And some leaf mulch at the Takoma city works yard.
Planted and dug for many hours.

It was a day to myself.
One young woman staying with me was off interviewing
U.S. Army veterans at a bikers'gathering in Gettysburg.
A second one fresh from the offices of the European Union
in Brussels arrives Tuesday.
So I enjoy the time alone.

Yesterday I visited some friends in Leisure World, a
retirement community about half an hour from here.
One active Lithuanian couple in their nineties, to share
some interesting items I'd found in my father's papers.
Another active Lithuanian couple, in their seventies, who
help me so much with my community affairs.
I lean on and learn from "the elders."
I feel so fortunate to be able to tap into their expertise.
Especially when history threatens to repeat itself.

Subject: Diana's Detour 217
Mon Jun 23, 2014

*"Tonight is Midsummer Night's Eve, also called St. John's Eve.
St. John is the patron saint of beekeepers. It's a time when the hives
are full of honey. The full moon that occurs this month was called
the Mead Moon, because honey was fermented to make mead, and
that's where the word "honeymoon" comes from. It is a time for
lovers. An old Swedish proverb says, "Midsummer Night is not
long but it sets many cradles rocking.*

*Shakespeare set his play A Midsummer Night's Dream on this
night. It tells the story of two young couples who wander into a
magical forest outside Athens. In the play, Shakespeare wrote,
"The course of true love never did run smooth.""*

The above info is from Garrison Keillor. Lithuanians take "Joninės," the feast of St. John which occurs on the same night, very seriously, too. There are celebrations next weekend at Swain's lock on the C&O Canal, and a major festival in New Jersey, not to speak of what goes on in Lithuania, where it doesn't get dark until around midnight. Jumping over bonfires, weaving wreaths from wildflowers then setting them off into water, lots of singing under the stars. And to think, as of tomorrow, we head back toward autumn....

Subject: Diana's Detour 218
Tue, Jun 24, 2014

Any time I am home on a weekday in the summertime,
I feel like I'm twelve years old again.
Adults somewhere are in charge of my world.
All I have to worry about is what book I want to read.
How much Hawaiian Tropic Tanning Oil to slather on.
Getting the lawn mowed and the petunias watered.
Peeling some potatoes for dinner or getting the table set.
Hoping my mother will take us to the pool when she gets home from work.

There is certainly a lot of noise at home during the day.
Trees being taken down.
Hammering and construction.
Dogs barking.
Horns honking.
Birds bickering.

Time seems to be so full yet goes by so quickly.
Today feels and sounds just like a summer day 50 years ago.

My port was removed today!
I am officially device-free.
The last vestige of my cancer treatment is gone, gone, gone.
I believe they call it an "extirpation."

The procedure itself took about 10 minutes early this morning.
I chose Novocain over sedation so I could talk to the doctor while he was working on me.
The tugging I felt, apart from the area below my right clavicle being opened up, was the surgeon pulling the skin away from the device it had become attached to, or grown a scar shield around.

I asked to look at it. Removed and cleaned up, it was a small purple triangular device, with a very long (6 inch?) thin white tube attached. The tube had been in my heart's right ventricle for the past 7 months, allowing various medications and poisons to be pumped into my veins to get rid of any lingering cancer cells in my body.

The port is your best friend during chemotherapy. It allows you to be pricked only once, and your veins don't burn the way they sometimes can with IVs in the arms or hands.
Good-bye, old friend.

Good-bye, old cancer.
I didn't fight you.
I accepted you, hosted you, but now it was time for you to go.

I want to pause now and thank everyone who prayed for me.
I know many of my friends don't believe in God, but their good wishes I consider to be prayers.

But for those who have prayed to God on my behalf, many, many thanks.
It has worked. Amen.

Sometimes that is all one can do, and those of us who have learned to pray do call upon God in times of need.
And those who are true believers pray in all times, keeping their relationship with God open and nurtured.

Blaise Pascal (of "Pascal's Wager") wrote, "In faith there is enough light for those who want to believe and enough shadows to blind those who don't."

He spent much of his life in conflict between science and religion, and was one of the first philosophers to seriously question the existence of God. But in 1654, he experienced a revelation, the account of which he carried sewn into his coat lining until his death. He came to the conclusion that there was no science to prove the existence of God, but that humans must rely on their faith. He said, "The heart has its reasons which reason knows nothing of."

A child prodigy (born in 1623), by the time he was 19 he had already perfected the first mechanical calculator for sale to the public. In the field of physics, he discovered that air has weight, and he conducted experiments to prove that vacuums could exist, which led him to formulate the hydraulic principle that "pressure exerted on a fluid in a closed vessel is transmitted unchanged throughout the fluid." This principle is used today in devices such as syringes, hydraulic presses, automobile brakes, and aircraft controls. In mathematics, he founded the theory of probabilities and developed an early form of integral calculus.

Pascal's last scientific effort was the design of a public transit system for the city of Paris, which was instituted in 1662, the same year that he died, at the age of thirty-nine. **[BTW, I get this info from Garrison Keillor's Writer's Almanac]**

	God exists	*God does not exist*
Wager for God	Gain all	Status quo
Wager against God	Misery	Status quo

Wagering for God superdominates wagering against God: the worst outcome associated with wagering for God (status quo) is at least as good as the best outcome associated with wagering against God (status quo); and if God exists, the result of wagering for God is strictly better that the result of wagering against God. (The fact that the result is much better does not matter yet.) Pascal draws the conclusion at this point that rationality requires you to wager for God.

For those who wagered that God exists, thank you for your prayers.
Whether he does or not, they were answered.

Subject: Diana's Detour 219
Wed, Jun 25, 2014

My daughter said it was too soon to ask people to stop praying for me.
That it wasn't over yet.
That the cancer could still come back.

I know that, but I feel like the first three-month scan gave me a new lease on life.
It meant that my decision not to get the radiation did not doom me.
It gave me a breather.

Rather than focus on wrapping things up, I have a little (perhaps a lot!) more time left.
Deadlines (what a word!) stress me, energize me, but it seems I can never meet them fully.

Tonight's explosive thunderstorm (what lightning! what thunder! what a downpour!) reminded me that I'd always wanted to die in a natural disaster. So long as there was no fire, drowning, or suffocation involved....

A year or two ago in the Washington area, there had been the report of a man who was sitting in his Mercedes at a stop sign when an oak tree fell on his car, killing him instantly.
To me, that sounded like a perfect way to leave this world.

Getting cancer was like being struck by lightning, a bolt out of the blue.
In a way, it made you feel special, like a selected one.
It never made me feel sorry for myself.

I guess that's where the denial comes in.

I keep thinking I can get an extension on that deadline.

Subject: Diana's Detour 220
Thurs, Jun 26, 2014

The body is amazing in its ability to heal.
I am thinking that now, once my most current cut heals, and my hair grows long enough for me to shed the wig and sweat a lot, I should go back to doing boot camp.

I feel like I owe it to my body to repay it for helping me get through this.
I want to make sure I have the ability to do so again.
Plus, I still aspire to have Michelle Obama arms.....

Subject: Re: Diana's Detour 221
Friday, Jun 27, 2014

My children's grandmother on their father's side once recited this sweet saying.
I think it was something she had learned as a child, because she said she no longer believed in God after living through World War II.
"Aš ne lapas atpūstas, bet Dievulio atsiųstas."
"I am not a leaf randomly blown here by the wind; I was purposely sent by God."

VII from This Day[43]
by Wendell Berry (b. 1934)

Again I resume the long
lesson: how small a thing
can be pleasing, how little
in this hard world it takes
to satisfy the mind
and bring it to its rest.

Within the ongoing havoc
the woods this morning is
almost unnaturally still.
Through stalled air, unshadowed
light, a few leaves fall
of their own weight.

The sky
is gray. It begins in mist
almost at the ground
and rises forever. The trees
rise in silence almost
natural, but not quite,
almost eternal, but
not quite.

What more did I
think I wanted? Here is
what has always been.
Here is what will always
be. Even in me,
the Maker of all this
returns in rest, even
to the slightest of His works,
a yellow leaf slowly
falling, and is pleased.

Subject: Diana's Detour 222
Saturday, June 28, 2014

We've made the shift.
Toward Autumn.
Imperceptible but true.
It doesn't seem right that the first official day of summer coincides with the summer solstice.
But look around, and everything that was going to be blooming already is.
Or is prepared to.
Even the chrysanthemums have buds on them
If you haven't pruned them.
And my lone sunflower is 6 feet tall.
No head on it yet, but too late to start one from seed.

Illinois[44]
Philip F. Deaver (b. 1946)

I recall a catbird on the wire
between my house and the corner pole
and the dense green maple leaves
and the grass growing fast below
and the peonies, tulips, the sidewalks
stretching down each block to my friends,
and from out of the houses, the voices
of neighbors camped nearby for life,
those close to us in spirit,
those held at arms length, and they us,
and I know when I recall this bird
dancing on our phone line and
singing upwards toward a mate
invisible in the waving treetops,

that it isn't exactly the bird I'm remembering
but the slant of light and the swell
of humid Illinois summer
pressing in around her.

Subject: Diana's Detour 223
Sunday, Jun 29 2014

To everything there is a season.

I found the handmade card my daughter had put into the chemo bag she had prepared for me when I was just getting started with the detour. She had written out the following, and circled the word "healing."

Ecclesiastes 3
King James Version (KJV)[45]
¹ *To every thing there is a season, and a time to every purpose under the heaven:*
² *A time to be born, and a time to die; a time to plant, and a time to pluck up that which is planted;*
³ *A time to kill, and a time to heal; a time to break down, and a time to build up;*
⁴ *A time to weep, and a time to laugh; a time to mourn, and a time to dance;*
⁵ *A time to cast away stones, and a time to gather stones together; a time to embrace, and a time to refrain from embracing;*
⁶ *A time to get, and a time to lose; a time to keep, and a time to cast away;*
⁷ *A time to rend, and a time to sew; a time to keep silence, and a time to speak;*
⁸ *A time to love, and a time to hate; a time of war, and a time of peace.*

Subject: Diana's Detour 224
Monday, June 30, 2014

"Cancer changes your life, often for the better. You learn what's important, you learn to prioritize, and you learn not to waste your time. You tell people you love them." My friend Gilda Radner (who died of ovarian cancer in 1989 at age 42) used to say, 'If it wasn't for the downside, having cancer would be the best thing and everyone would want it.' That's true. If it wasn't for the downside."

-Excerpted from PEOPLE Weekly's August 6, 2001 issue. - Joel Siegel, Good Morning America movie critic (1943-2007)

Subject: Diana's Detour 225
Tuesday, Jul 1, 2014

If I could count the hours I've spent in fluorescent-lit offices
shut off from any sight or scent of the outside
I am afraid it would add up to years
Perhaps decades.

That does sound sad.
Me and a computer.
A typewriter in the early years.
And then there was Wang.

What I wouldn't give for a good Selectric today.
Forms we used to type up, we do again by hand.

So while the US soccer team was trying to hold its own against the Belgians,

I proofread bills for major clients, quibbling over whether the discounted rate was $710 or $711/hour.

Then I came home.
The sun was still out.
But the mosquitoes were vicious already.
So I went in and let the day end on its own.

We could use a good thunderstorm.

Subject: Diana's Detour 226
Wed, Jul 2, 2014

Dyed my half inch of grey hair blonde,
so I no longer look just like my 90-year old mother.
But I still appear pretty androgynous
With the beginnings of a mullet.

It's hard not to ditch the wig when it's 98 outside but "feels like 108."
However, my fluorescent-lit life is also comfortably air-conditioned.

We are in the throes of hurricane Arthur anticipation.
To add some reality-show drama to our everyday lives.
I hope it doesn't affect my 5:45 pm departure today for Cincinnati.

Once again, I will miss the 4th of July festivities in Our Nation's Capital.
And our eccentric 4th of July parade here in Takoma Park

With the dueling reel mowers, and Caribbean Tin Drum Bands.
Not to speak of our own impressively loud and crowded evening fireworks display.

It will actually be cooler in the Midwest.
And Cincinnati's Ohio River fireworks display is spectacular.
I remember when it was timed to music,
And we held our transistor radios to our ears for the symphonic accompaniment.

Ah, the days of low technology....

Here follows the "Art is long, and Time is fleeting" poem
(although Hippocrates said it first)
..... So be in the present

A Psalm of Life (1838)[46]
Henry Wadsworth Longfellow (1807-1882)

What the heart of the young man
Said to the Psalmist
Tell me not, in mournful numbers,
Life is but an empty dream! —
For the soul is dead that slumbers,
And things are not what they seem.
Life is real! Life is earnest!
And the grave is not its goal;
Dust thou art, to dust returnest,
Was not spoken of the soul.
Not enjoyment, and not sorrow,
Is our destined end or way;
But to act, that each to-morrow

Find us farther than to-day.
Art is long, and Time is fleeting,
And our hearts, though stout and brave,
Still, like muffled drums, are beating
Funeral marches to the grave.
In the world's broad field of battle,
In the bivouac of Life,
Be not like dumb, driven cattle!
Be a hero in the strife!
Trust no Future, howe'er pleasant!
Let the dead Past bury its dead!
Act, — act in the living Present!
Heart within, and God o'erhead!
Lives of great men all remind us
We can make our lives sublime,
And, departing, leave behind us
Footprints on the sands of time;
Footprints, that perhaps another,
Sailing o'er life's solemn main,
A forlorn and shipwrecked brother,
Seeing, shall take heart again.
Let us, then, be up and doing,
With a heart for any fate;
Still achieving, still pursuing,
Learn to labor and to wait.

Subject: Diana's Detour 227
Thurs, July 3, 2014

Some thoughts for the Fourth of July.
After 4 hours at the airport and a cancelled flight, I may still
get to Cincinnati before midnight.

For anyone who has not been to the Library of Congress in Washington, DC, a palatial spectacle awaits you. Just as one doesn't expect City Hall in San Francisco to resemble a cathedral, who would expect such dazzling beauty in a library?

And as she states in this poem "Where else in all America are we so symbolized / As in this hall?"

From *The Congressional Library*[47]
Amy Lowell (published in *The Literary Digest*, 1922)

The earth is a colored thing.
See the red clays, and the umbers and salt greasy of the
*   mountains;*
See the clustered and wandering greens of plains and hillsides,
The leaf-greens, bush-greens, water-plant and snow-greens
Of gardens and forests.
See the reds of flowers — hibiscus, poppy, geranium;
The rose-red of little flowers — may-flowers, primroses;
The harlequin shades of sweet-peas, orchids, pansies;
The madders, saffrons, chromes, of still waters,
The silver and star-blues, the wine-blues of seas and oceans.
Observe the stars at nighttime, name the color of them;
Count and recount the hues of clouds at sunset and at dawn.
And the colors of the races of men —
What are they?
And what are we?
We, the people without a race,
Without a language;
Of all races, and of none;
Of all tongues, and one imposed;

Of all traditions and all pasts,
With no tradition and no past.
A patchwork and an altar-piece,
Vague as sea-mist,
Myriad as forest-trees,
Living into a present,
Building a future.
Our color is the vari-colored world.
No colors clash,
All clash and change,
And, in changing, new colors come and go and dominate and
     remain,
And no one shall say which remain,
Since those that have vanished return,
And those no man has seen take the light and are.

Where else in all America are we so symbolized
As in this hall?
White columns polished like glass,
A dome and a dome,
A balcony and a balcony,
Stairs and the balustrades to them,
Yellow marble and red slabs of it,
All mounting, spearing, flying into color.
Color round the dome and up to it,
Color curving, kite-flying, to the second dome,
Light, dropping, pitching down upon the color,
Arrow-falling upon the glass-bright pillars,
Mingled colors spinning into a shape of white pillars,
Fusing, cooling, into balanced shafts of shrill and
     interthronging light.
This is America,
This vast, confused beauty,
This staring, restless speed of loveliness,

Mighty, overwhelming, crude, of all forms,
Making grandeur out of profusion,
Afraid of no incongruities,
Sublime in its audacity,
Bizarre breaker of moulds,
Laughing with strength,
Charging down on the past,
Glorious and conquering,
Destroyer, builder,
Invincible pith and marrow of the world,
An old world remaking,
Whirling into the no-world of all-colored light.

Subject: Diana's Detour 228
Fri, July 4, 2014

Good Night (from Smoke and Steel, 1920)[48]
by Carl Sandburg (1878-1967)
Many ways to say good night.

Fireworks at a pier on the Fourth of July
  spell it with red wheels and yellow spokes.
They fizz in the air, touch the water and quit.
Rockets make a trajectory of gold-and-blue
  and then go out.

Railroad trains at night spell with a smokestack mushrooming a
  white pillar.

Steamboats turn a curve in the Mississippi crying a baritone
  that crosses lowland cottonfields to razorback hill.

It is easy to spell good night.
  Many ways to spell good night.

Subject: Diana's Detour 229 and 230
Sun, July 6, 2014

When I fly into Washington, DC, I am always reminded
what a beautiful city I live in.
And today was no exception.

And then, when I step off the metro at the Takoma Platform,
I am stunned by the verdant view.
Low houses sunken in oak and pine and magnolia and
rhododendron.

A view of verdure that may soon be gone
once they throw up a six-story apartment building
In the middle of the metro parking lot
And eliminate any view of green and trees from the
platform.

No one considers the value of a view.
Except the early planners of Washington, DC,
Who insisted that no building would exceed twelve stories
in height
So that the Capitol building would be visible from
everywhere.

How does one measure that?
How can one enter that as a line item in a development
project?

I came across this poem, and I liked that Washington had
an eccentric at its creation.
And now I know who Banneker High School is named after.

Banneker[49]
By Rita Dove (b. 1952)

What did he do except lie
under a pear tree, wrapped in
a great cloak, and meditate
on the heavenly bodies?
Venerable, the good people of Baltimore
whispered, shocked and more than
a little afraid. After all it was said
he took to strong drink.
Why else would he stay out
under the stars all night
and why hadn't he married?
But who would want him! Neither
Ethiopian nor English, neither
lucky nor crazy, a capacious bird
humming as he penned in his mind
another enflamed letter
to President Jefferson—he imagined
the reply, polite and rhetorical.
Those who had been to Philadelphia
reported the statue
of Benjamin Franklin
before the library
his very size and likeness.
A wife? No, thank you.
At dawn he milked
the cows, then went inside
and put on a pot to stew
while he slept. The clock
he whittled as a boy
still ran. Neighbors
woke him up

with warm bread and quilts.
At nightfall he took out
his rifle — a white-maned
figure stalking the darkened
breast of the Union — and
shot at the stars, and by chance
one went out. Had he killed?
I assure thee, my dear Sir!
Lowering his eyes to fields
sweet with the rot of spring, he could see
a government's domed city
rising from the morass and spreading
in a spiral of lights....

NOTES: Benjamin Banneker (1731-1806), first black man to devise an almanac and predict a solar eclipse accurately, was also appointed to the commission that surveyed and laid out what is now Washington, D.C.

Subject: Diana's Detour 231 an 232
Tues, July 8, 2014

I don't know what to think or do about those thousands of poor unaccompanied immigrant children from Guatemala and Honduras being dumped on the US border with Mexico.
Their parents inspired by a George Bush-era law (blaming Obama now, of course), thinking the US has given them blanket permission to come.
Coyote smugglers making a fortune by dumping those children and going back to get more.
Who's not going to take in a child?

No need to transport them more deeply into the US, as one would with adults.
Even my mother thinks it's an Obama plan to have Africans and Indians take over the U.S.

- Whether one is rich or poor,
educated or illiterate,
religious or non believing,
man or woman,
black, white, or brown,
we are all the same.
Physically, emotionally, and mentally, we are all equal.
We all share basic needs for food, ...shelter, safety, and love.
We all aspire to happiness and we all shun suffering.
Each of us has hopes, worries, fears, and dreams.
Each of us wants the best for our family and loved ones.
We all experience pain when we suffer loss and joy when we
*   achieve what we seek.*
On this fundamental level, religion, ethnicity, culture, and
*   language make no difference.*

—Dalai Lama[50]

Subject: Diana's Detour 233
Wed, Jul 9, 2014

"I'll bet it's heat from the oven. Have you baked anything lately?"
That was the conclusion of the friend I was visiting, who has also been visited by cancer recently.
We were comparing wig issues and conveniences.

I removed mine, and she clucked "No, not yet. It makes you look much too old"
Even though I've dyed my grey hair blonde.
Androgynous, I knew, but old?

It's the shortness. I still look like a recovering cancer patient.
It's been four months since my chemotherapy ended.
Hair that seems to grow fast when you have lots of it takes forever to get to a basic length.
I don't mind the "gamin" look, and have worn my hair very short before.
But never down to the scalp.

Its like starting seedlings.
They sprout, but seem to take forever to get to the point where you can transplant them and then grow them to fullness.

I was hoping my hair would grow out enough that I could go "au naturel" in Lithuania at the end of August.
But a half-inch of growth is not going to make enough of a difference.

Back on with the wig.

But the wig is doing something funny.
Right up front, right where it's most visible, the hairs have become frizzy and coarse.
I brush and I brush and I can't brush them straight.

I couldn't understand this sudden phenomenon.
Until my friend mentioned baking.

You know the way your eyebrows sometimes feel singed
when you open a hot oven.
Apparently, wigs don't react well to heat, either.

I'll blame the strawberry-rhubarb pie I made Monday night.
It was still worth it.

Subject: Re: Diana's Detour 234
Thur, Jul 10, 2014

No sooner did I walk outside and see the storm clouds
gathering up Connecticut Avenue
than I turned right back into my office building to get an
umbrella.
And I'm so glad I did.
By the time the metro reached Takoma, it was pouring
down rain.

I must admit, I am a great fan of umbrellas, giant ones.
There is a school of thought that hates umbrellas.
Don't ask me why.
I feel so liberated and comfortable
and really enjoy walking in the rain
When I have an umbrella for a roof.

Instead of squinting against the raindrops
My eyes are wide open to the wonders of the wet world.

Takoma was enclosed in a complete rainbow Tuesday
evening.
I believe it was a double.
Missed it. Saw it on Facebook and made it my new
background picture on my profile page.

Subject: Diana's Detour 235
Fri, Jul 11, 2014

I've always liked this poem
Imperfection as beauty.
A chaos of color.

Freckles in some cultures were considered a defect.
There's an old Lithuanian "cure" for freckles that uses ant urine.
Just throw a white handkerchief onto an anthill, it is said, and the ants will pee all over it.
Then place said dampened handkerchief upon face.
Freckles should disappear (I have not tried this as I like my freckles, so I cannot vouch for the advice).

Pied Beauty[51]
by Gerard Manley Hopkins

Glory be to God for dappled things —
For skies of couple-colour as a brindled cow;
For rose-moles all in stipple upon trout that swim;
Fresh-firecoal chestnut-falls; finches' wings;
Landscape plotted and pieced—fold, fallow, and plough;
And all trades, their gear and tackle and trim.
All things counter, original, spare, strange;
Whatever is fickle, freckled (who knows how?)
With swift, slow; sweet, sour; adazzle, dim;
He fathers-forth whose beauty is past change:
Praise him.

Subject: Re: Diana's Detour 236
Sat, Jul 12, 2014

There's a beautiful full moon out tonight.
It should become a super moon closer to dawn.

It's 75 degrees, breezy, with very low humidity.
An unusually pleasant evening for DC in the summertime.

I have friends who are at the beach this weekend.
If it's lovely here, it must be wonderful there.

My next-door neighbor chatted me up as I was removing
vines this evening.
The wisteria, the autumn clematis, the porcelain berry, and
just plain English ivy.
I have to dig it out of the bark of the elm, out of the six-foot
high chain link fence between us,
And off the red brick of my house.
It actually gets through the windows, and the next thing
you know, I have 4 feet of ivy growing in my basement.

He's the neighbor who hates the overhanging trees.
My elm, he says, will fall on his house.
It shades his entire yard.
And the half-dead oak of my neighbor up the hill will fall
onto mine.

My visiting Lithuanian girls are shocked that we live among
such tall, old trees.
It was back in 1989, when my son was a newborn, that
storms tore through this area
And Washington lost one third of all its old growth trees.

We do live in danger, I suppose, but their shade and the rustling of their leaves and
the sheer green mass of their presence make it worth it.
They hush our world, soften it, color it, and help the wind lull us to sleep.
I hear no birds or cicadas tonight.
Just the music of leaves moving loudly, then softly, then loudly again.

Subject: Diana's Detour 237
Sunday, July 13, 2014

Rain in Summer[52]
Henry Wadsworth Longfellow

How beautiful is the rain!
After the dust and heat,
In the broad and fiery street,
In the narrow lane,
How beautiful is the rain!
How it clatters along the roofs,
Like the tramp of hoofs
How it gushes and struggles out
From the throat of the overflowing spout!
Across the window-pane
It pours and pours;
And swift and wide,
With a muddy tide,
Like a river down the gutter roars
The rain, the welcome rain!

The sick man from his chamber looks
At the twisted brooks;
He can feel the cool
Breath of each little pool;
His fevered brain
Grows calm again,
And he breathes a blessing on the rain.

From the neighboring school
Come the boys,
With more than their wonted noise
And commotion;
And down the wet streets
Sail their mimic fleets,
Till the treacherous pool
Ingulfs them in its whirling
And turbulent ocean.

In the country, on every side,
Where far and wide,
Like a leopard's tawny and spotted hide,
Stretches the plain,
To the dry grass and the drier grain
How welcome is the rain!

In the furrowed land
The toilsome and patient oxen stand;
Lifting the yoke encumbered head,
With their dilated nostrils spread,
They silently inhale
The clover-scented gale,
And the vapors that arise
From the well-watered and smoking soil.

For this rest in the furrow after toil
Their large and lustrous eyes
Seem to thank the Lord,
More than man's spoken word.

Near at hand,
From under the sheltering trees,
The farmer sees
His pastures, and his fields of grain,
As they bend their tops
To the numberless beating drops
Of the incessant rain.
He counts it as no sin
That he sees therein
Only his own thrift and gain.

These, and far more than these,
The Poet sees!
He can behold
Aquarius old
Walking the fenceless fields of air;
And from each ample fold
Of the clouds about him rolled
Scattering everywhere
The showery rain,
As the farmer scatters his grain.

He can behold
Things manifold
That have not yet been wholly told, —
Have not been wholly sung nor said.
For his thought, that never stops,
Follows the water-drops

Down to the graves of the dead,
Down through chasms and gulfs profound,
To the dreary fountain-head
Of lakes and rivers under ground;
And sees them, when the rain is done,
On the bridge of colors seven
Climbing up once more to heaven,
Opposite the setting sun.

Thus the Seer,
With vision clear,
Sees forms appear and disappear,
In the perpetual round of strange,
Mysterious change
From birth to death, from death to birth,
From earth to heaven, from heaven to earth;
Till glimpses more sublime
Of things, unseen before,
Unto his wondering eyes reveal
The Universe, as an immeasurable wheel
Turning forevermore
In the rapid and rushing river of Time.

Subject: Diana's 238
Mon, Jul 14, 2014

Willie Nelson sings it, but so has Ella Fitzgerald, Frank
Sinatra, Lyle Lovett, and Rosemary Clooney, to name a very
few.
I thought Hoagy Carmichael had written it, but it was
actually Irving Berlin in 1926, who in 1941 wrote "White

Christmas" several days after the Japanese attack on Pearl Harbor.

In 1927, "Blue Skies" became one of the first songs to be featured in a talkie, when Al Jolson performed it in The Jazz Singer.

"Blue Skies"[53]
Music and words by Irving Berlin

Blue skies smilin' at me
Nothin' but blue skies do I see
Bluebirds singin' a song
Nothin' but bluebirds all day long.
Never saw the sun shinin' so bright
Never saw things goin' so right
Noticing the days hurrying by
When you're in love, my how they fly.
Blue days, all of them gone
Nothin' but blue skies from now on

Subject: Diana's Detour 239
Tues, Jul 15, 2014

Storm Ending[54]
Jean Toomer (1922)

Thunder blossoms gorgeously above our heads,
Great, hollow, bell-like flowers,
Rumbling in the wind,
Stretching clappers to strike our ears . . .
Full-lipped flowers
Bitten by the sun
Bleeding rain
Dripping rain like golden honey—
And the sweet earth flying from the thunder.

Subject: Diana's Detour 240
Wed, July 16, 2014

A month from now, I will be getting on a plane bound for Lithuania, to take a version of the trip I had planned to take last October, before cancer paid its surprise visit.

The downside is that the October 2013 trip was an unrepeatable "reunion of the cousins," including my brother from Ann Arbor and many cousins in Lithuania, from Kazlų Rūda to Kalvarija. It also involved a tour of historic and literary places that would have meant a lot to me.

The upside of the "consolation" trip in August is that it will include my daughter and her boyfriend! It was actually their trip, but they asked me to join them, so I am shocked and more than happy to. I also get to plan the itinerary and interface with the adults.

I am still awed by the amazing power of the body to heal, of life to get back to normal, and of selective poisons administered expertly to slay the dragon that dwelt within.

Subject: Diana's Detour 241
Thurs, July 17, 2014

I was a little surprised a few weeks ago when my daughter sent me her flight information for their onward travel to Europe after Lithuania.
They're taking Vilnius to Rome, via Kiev, on Ukrainian Airlines.
Having flown Aeroflot back in the day, I would not have booked on Ukrainian airlines.
With a stop in Kiev?

But adventure is adventure.
Until today.
When a Malaysian airliner got shot down over Ukraine, with 297 aboard, 80 of them children.
That's not adventure anymore. That's war.

Subject: Diana's Detour 242
Friday, July 18, 2014

A Boat, Beneath a Sunny Sky[55]
Lewis Carroll 1832-1898

A boat, beneath a sunny sky
Lingering onward dreamily
In an evening of July —
Children three that nestle near,
Eager eye and willing ear,
Pleased a simple tale to hear —
Long has paled that sunny sky:
Echoes fade and memories die:
Autumn frosts have slain July.

Still she haunts me, phantomwise,
Alice moving under skies
Never seen by waking eyes.

Children yet, the tale to hear,
Eager eye and willing ear,
Lovingly shall nestle near.

In a Wonderland they lie,
Dreaming as the days go by,
Dreaming as the summers die:
Ever drifting down the stream —
Lingering in the golden gleam —
Life, what is it but a dream?

Subject: Diana's Detour 243
Saturday, July 19 2014

We just want all of our daughters (and sons) (and grandchildren, should we live so long to see any!) to have a happy life....

I Meet My Grandmother in Italy[56]
by Katrina Vandenberg

I find her where I least expect her,
Santa Marguerita, with yellow roses
in her hair. She laughs, deep

in the arms of that American GI,
her hair rolled like Hepburn's, her lipstick
red as tiled Verona roofs. Then I remember

the Saturday before she died, the way
we stopped at a greenhouse and she said,
I'll take for my granddaughter all

the plants you have with yellow flowers,
ignoring my protests until the Pontiac
was heaped with roses and verbena,

with lemon gladiola perfume I could gather
in my hands. She said, Take them
all; you need to have a happy life.

Subject: Diana's Detour 244
Sun July 20, 2014

How does one tell young people today that there are no
certainties in life.
That expecting to be 100% sure about a decision is like
demanding proof of the existence of God.
That's where a leap of faith comes in.

That experience is overrated.
That you are never so wise as when you act with a pure
heart.
That the choices made in your twenties determine the
course of the rest of your days.
That what seems tedious and mundane today will seem
precious and irreplaceable once it's gone.

Sometimes, I think we live too long.
If life were short, and dangerous, we wouldn't think about
every step so much.
We would be bold, and not think twice, because we
wouldn't have the time to.

"The greatest generation" had the opportunity to be heroic.
The Depression. A world war. Life whittled down to bare
necessities.
It's much harder to be great and make bold choices in a time
of calm and plenty.
When you have many choices, not one or two, they all seem
compelling.
So confusing.
An embarrassment of riches.

But still, we write our own life story, no matter what the circumstances.
And we live out the outline we lay down when we were young.

Subject: Re: Diana's Detour 245
Mon, Jul 21, 2014

There's nothing like a two-hour conference call in the evening after a full day of work.
At least I got grocery shopping done and dinner made beforehand.

Now I have an editorial to write, and a campaign to set in motion connecting the crisis in Ukraine with the 25th anniversary of the Baltic Way that took place on August 23, 1989, to highlight the Molotov Ribbentrop agreement signed 60 years before on August 23, 1939 that started WWII.
My creative juices are already flowing.

There's a conference I'll have to attend in LA Oct 10-12.
And my 45th high school reunion in Cincinnati will also be in October.

I can't believe I'll be able to go to those events!
Last year I was on the operating table Oct 9.
What a difference a year makes.

Subject: Diana's 246
Tues, Jul 22, 2014

A beautiful poem... by a Baltimorean...

"Annabel Lee"[57]
Edgar Allan Poe (1809-1849)

It was many and many a year ago,
In a kingdom by the sea,
That a maiden there lived whom you may know
By the name of Annabel Lee;
And this maiden she lived with no other thought
Than to love and be loved by me.

I was a child and she was a child,
In this kingdom by the sea,
But we loved with a love that was more than love—
I and my Annabel Lee—
With a love that the wingèd seraphs of Heaven
Coveted her and me.

And this was the reason that, long ago,
In this kingdom by the sea,
A wind blew out of a cloud, chilling
My beautiful Annabel Lee;
So that her highborn kinsmen came
And bore her away from me,
To shut her up in a sepulchre
In this kingdom by the sea.

The angels, not half so happy in Heaven,
Went envying her and me—
Yes!—that was the reason (as all men know,

In this kingdom by the sea)
That the wind came out of the cloud by night,
Chilling and killing my Annabel Lee.

But our love it was stronger by far than the love
Of those who were older than we—
Of many far wiser than we—
And neither the angels in Heaven above
Nor the demons down under the sea
Can ever dissever my soul from the soul
Of the beautiful Annabel Lee;
For the moon never beams, without bringing me dreams
Of the beautiful Annabel Lee;
And the stars never rise, but I feel the bright eyes
Of the beautiful Annabel Lee;
And so, all the night-tide, I lie down by the side
Of my darling—my darling—my life and my bride,
In her sepulchre there by the sea—
In her tomb by the sounding sea

Subject: Diana's Detour 247
Wed, July 23, 2014

Young and Old[58]
Charles Kingsley (1819–1875)

When all the world is young, lad,
And all the trees are green;
And every goose a swan, lad,
And every lass a queen;
Then hey for boot and horse, lad,

And round the world away;
Young blood must have its course, lad,
And every dog his day.

When all the world is old, lad,
And all the trees are brown;
And all the sport is stale, lad,
And all the wheels run down:
Creep home, and take your place there,
The spent and maimed among:
God grant you find one face there
You loved when all was young.

From The Water-Babies. 1862

Subject: Diana's Detour 248
Thursday, July 24, 2014

I'm beginning to look like David Bowie.
So I think I am going to need a new wig until my hair reaches a decent length.
The fact that it's growing in curly doesn't help either.

I started wearing the original wig again when the front of the second one got fried after I opened an oven door.
The first one is blonde, too, but it has a dark cap, which I didn't notice when I bought it.
If I don't let the hair fall in my eyes, it looks like I'm wearing a headband.

I have just completed the second season of "Orange is the New Black."

In the last episode, an inmate with cancer and only weeks to live manages to break out, just so she doesn't have to die in prison.

The desperate rage of the wise, the good, the wild, and the grave against death can be found in Dylan Thomas's poem:

Do Not Go Gentle Into That Good Night[59]
Dylan Thomas (1914-1953)

Do not go gentle into that good night,
Old age should burn and rave at close of day;
Rage, rage against the dying of the light.

Though wise men at their end know dark is right,
Because their words had forked no lightning they
Do not go gentle into that good night.

Good men, the last wave by, crying how bright
Their frail deeds might have danced in a green bay,
Rage, rage against the dying of the light.

Wild men who caught and sang the sun in flight,
And learn, too late, they grieved it on its way,
Do not go gentle into that good night.

Grave men, near death, who see with blinding sight
Blind eyes could blaze like meteors and be gay,
Rage, rage against the dying of the light.

And you, my father, there on that sad height,
Curse, bless, me now with your fierce tears, I pray.
Do not go gentle into that good night.
Rage, rage against the dying of the light.

Subject: Diana's 249
Fri, Jul 25, 2014

An outstandingly beautiful day today.
The kind we rarely get in DC in mid July.
Took a walk around my office neighborhood at lunch.

White House looking good.
Washington Monument still there
Red begonias all over.
Trees thick with welcome shade.

This truly is a stunning city. In a spare, spacious way.

Sonnet LXXIII by William Shakespeare 1564-1616[60]

That time of year thou mayst in me behold
When yellow leaves, or none, or few, do hang
Upon those boughs which shake against the cold,
Bare ruin'd choirs, where late the sweet birds sang.
In me thou see'st the twilight of such day
As after sunset fadeth in the west;
Which by and by black night doth take away,
Death's second self, that seals up all in rest
In me thou see'st the glowing of such fire,
That on the ashes of his youth doth lie,
As the death-bed whereon it must expire
Consum'd with that which it was nourish'd by.

This thou perceiv'st, which makes thy love more strong,
To love that well which thou must leave ere long.

Subject: Diana's Detour 250
Sat, Jul 26, 2014

Here I am, having Sangria and Peruvian chicken with
friends outside on a lovely summer night.
Having spent the day cleaning up a yard that I love,
And making lime meringue pie and brownies.
When I hear that my neighbor with cancer has died.

He passed away quietly, at home, surrounded by his wife
and two teenaged sons.
He was exhausted.

The last time I saw him, he burst into tears saying "I thought
I had a lot of time, but now I think I don't."

And he's younger than I am.

Our Jewish atheist Christmas caroling organizer.
Rest in peace, Philip.
You made a difference.

Subject: Diana's Detour 251
Sun, Jul 27, 2014

Egg whites!
I want the world to know, that should you suffer what I did,
the answer is raw egg whites.

In making the salsa verde for my Peruvian chicken, I had to
chop up fresh jalapeno peppers.
Which I had never done before.

I didn't know, you're supposed to wear gloves.

A half hour after chopping, my hands were on fire.
Naturally, I Googled "relief for hands after chopping jalapeno peppers"
And found an endless list of comments.

The first few recommended olive oil, yoghurt, calamine lotion.
Nothing worked.
Around the 20th comment, someone mentioned calling an emergency room
And being told there was nothing that could be done.
Wait 4-6 hours, and it will eventually wear off.

I was in agony. And awaiting company.
But the 43rd comment offered advice from a Sri Lankan lady.
Soak the hands in raw egg whites.

Immediate relief.

Whatever is in egg whites neutralized the capsaicin in the jalapeno peppers.
Who knew.
Thank you, Google.

And unnamed Sri Lankan lady.

Subject: Diana's Detour 252
Monday, July 28, 2014

Aldous Huxley's *Brave New World* (1932) is often compared with George Orwell's *Nineteen Eighty-Four* (1948), since they each offer a view of a dystopian future. Cultural critic Neil Postman spelled out the difference in his 1985 book *Amusing Ourselves to Death*:[61]

"What Orwell feared were those who would ban books.
What Huxley feared was that there would be no reason to ban a
    book, for there would be no one who wanted to read one.

Orwell feared those who would deprive us of information.
Huxley feared those who would give us so much that we would
    be reduced to passivity and egoism.

Orwell feared that the truth would be concealed from us.
Huxley feared the truth would be drowned in a sea of
    irrelevance.

Orwell feared we would become a captive culture.
Huxley feared we would become a trivial culture. ...

In short, Orwell feared that what we fear will ruin us.
Huxley feared that our desire will ruin us."

I think Huxley wins…

Subject: Diana's Detour 253 & 254
Wed, July 30, 2014

"When we step away from our high-stressed lives and step into nature, we get a shift. Physiologically, our brains and bodies change. We relax, and the quality of our thought changes.

A different brain network activates. That brain network is available for a completely different kind of quality of thought which is much more introspective and self-referential. Oftentimes it leads to feelings of connectedness and that can lead to innovative thoughts. Early humans seeking a place to call home and seeing a place overlooking the ocean or river realized that it makes them happy. They said, "This is good, this is right, this is safe and the place to survive and thrive."

From Marine biologist Wallace J. Nichols' book, *Blue Mind: The Surprising Science That Shows How Being Near, In, On, or Under Water Can Make You Happier, Healthier, More Connected, and Better at What You Do*

Nature swept into our high-stressed lives this week, bringing balmy ocean breezes onto the sidewalks of K Street. When was the last time we had a summer like this? Low humidity, temperatures in the 70s? But still sunny and bright. And the air so clean. You feel like you're on a mini-vacation just taking a walk at lunch. And, like a rising tide that lifts all ships, everyone's mood seems to be lifted, too.

Nature really is balm to the soul. The ringing of cicadas that plays in the background of summer evening conversations outside, when suddenly the earth seems to take a deep breath and let out a cool sigh, and the canopy of leaves overhead responds.

Subject: Re: Diana's Detour 255
Thur, Jul 31, 2014

"You loved us better when we were little," my children complain when I gush over some picture from their baby and toddler years. Not better, just differently. I mean, how could you not? Such characters! Such personalities, all bundled up in those tiny little bodies. What a huge responsibility, but what a rewarding one.

"In Memoriam" from Saving Singletrees. [62]
Leo Dangel (b. 1941)

In the early afternoon my mother
was doing the dishes. I climbed
onto the kitchen table, I suppose
to play, and fell asleep there.
I was drowsy and awake, though,
as she lifted me up, carried me
on her arms into the living room,
and placed me on the davenport,
but I pretended to be asleep
the whole time, enjoying the luxury—
was too big for such a privilege
and just old enough to form
my only memory of her carrying me.
She's still moving me to a softer place.

Subject: Diana's 256
Fri, Aug 1, 2014

In memoriam A.H.H. (Part XXVII)[63]
Alfred, Lord Tennyson, Poet Laureate (1809 - 1892)

I envy not in any moods,
The captive void of noble rage,
The linnet born within the cage,
That never knew the summer woods:
I envy not the beast that takes
His license in the field of time,
Unfetter'd by the sense of crime,
To whom a conscience never wakes;
Nor, what may count itself as blest,
The heart that never plighted troth
But stagnates in the weed of sloth;
Nor any want-begotten rest.
I hold it true, whate'er befall;
I feel it, when I sorrow most;
'Tis better to have loved and lost
Than never to have loved at all.

Subject: Diana's Detour 257
Saturday, Aug 2, 2014

O dead bumblebee, where is thy sting?
I find you curled up on your side on the wicker table
Beneath the bouquet of Black-Eyed Susans.

Drunk from the nectar?
Often, I see one like you immobile on a cushion of
pinkening sedum

Or stuck to a petal of phlox

Always so industrious
And yet,
Work hard, play hard?

Better to die a bacchanalian death in the open
Than huddled in a worker cube at the hive?
Or just overstayed the curfew of your 1-4 month life....

Subject: Diana's Detour 258
Sun, Aug 3, 2014

There's a Kenyan proverb: "When elephants fight, it's the grass that suffers."

WWI started 100 years ago this month. Actually, July 28, 1914. "The war to end all wars."

I am translating the first pages of a diary maintained by a 50 year old woman who lived out that war in the Lithuanian countryside, surrounded and intimidated by German and Russian soldiers in turn.

Her late father had been the local doctor, and their country home a gathering place for independence-minded activists and writers from all over Lithuania. She operated a pharmacy out of their home, which also served as a community information center, and a book-smuggling operation back when the Russian tsar forbade printing in the Lithuanian language.

Rather than going back to her editorial job in Vilnius or emigrating, she chose to stick out World War I among her rural neighbors, and her diary was later published in three volumes, yet to be translated into English. It offers a rare personal glimpse into the day-to-day experience of war as it descends upon a people, robbing them of their young men, their food, their security.

Collateral damage. The grass that suffers.

Subject: Re: Diana's Detour 259
Mon, Aug 4, 2014

There is no dawn chorus any more.
Only a mourning dove or a hoot owl with its plaintiff "oo-oo" at 5:15 am.
Autumn is a-cumin' in .
We still have the air conditioning off, but it may get warmer this week.

I believe I had nesting blue jays this summer.
They are often at the water tray atop my chimnea.

My new Amish picnic table and four benches were delivered today from Pennsylvania.
Beautiful fresh blond wood, actually chemically treated pine.
But thick, and heavy. 4' x 5'.
Hard to believe the old grey weathered table, picked up by some neighbors down the street, started out its life this fresh and pale.
I think I'll stain this one and try to preserve it.
Although 25 years was a pretty long life for an unstained table to last.

Subject: Diana's Detour 260
Tues, Aug 5, 2014

Ringing, buzzing, chittering, tinkling
The sounds of a summer night.
Nonstop, pulsating, rhythmically churning
Background, no, foreground, music not noise.

I wish I were by the ocean
And could hear the pounding waves
And the slurping surf.
Nonstop, pulsating, rhythmically churning.

But I have this
In the dry summer hills.
To remind me that we are not alone
And that we mean nothing to those who play this symphony.

Subject: Diana's Detour 261
Wed, Aug 6, 2014

It scares me how close Labor Day is.

Summer's Elegy[64]
Howard Nemerov (1920-1991)

Day after day, day after still day,
The summer has begun to pass away.
Starlings at twilight fly clustered and call,
And branches bend, and leaves begin to fall.
The meadow and the orchard grass are mown,
And the meadowlark's house is cut down.

The little lantern bugs have doused their fires,
The swallows sit in rows along the wires.
Berry and grape appear among the flowers
Tangled against the wall in secret bowers,
And cricket now begins to hum the hours
Remaining to the passion's slow procession
Down from the high place and the golden session
Wherein the sun was sacrificed for us.

A failing light, no longer numinous,
Now frames the long and solemn afternoons
Where butterflies regret their closed cocoons.
We reach the place unripe, and made to know
As with a sudden knowledge that we go
Away forever, all hope of return
Cut off, hearing the crackle of the burn-
ing blade behind us, and the terminal sound
Of apples dropping on the dry ground.

Subject: Diana's Detour 262
Thurs, Aug 7, 2014

I've made my fruit salad for 15, as requested, for tomorrow's funeral.
And I am just one of 10 doing so.
This is a group effort, by the Interfaith Family Project, "An independent community committed to sharing, learning about, and celebrating our Jewish and Christian traditions." My friend was Jewish and his wife is Catholic. He was concerned that, were he to be buried in a Jewish cemetery, as he wished, his wife would not be able to be buried here.

There are some famous lines in this (very long) poem.

And the more often I read it, the more my heart goes out to those many whose talents were never nurtured, whose lights were never given the opportunity to shine, whose minds did not reach the world to be able to contribute to it.

"Elegy Written in a Country Churchyard"[65] by Thomas Gray 1751

1   The curfew tolls the knell of parting day,
2   The lowing herd wind slowly o'er the lea,
3   The ploughman homeward plods his weary way,
4   And leaves the world to darkness and to me.

5   Now fades the glimmering landscape on the sight,
6   And all the air a solemn stillness holds,
7   Save where the beetle wheels his droning flight,
8   And drowsy tinklings lull the distant folds;

9   Save that from yonder ivy-mantled tower
10 The moping owl does to the moon complain
11 Of such, as wandering near her secret bower,
12 Molest her ancient solitary reign.

13 Beneath those rugged elms, that yew-tree's shade,
14 Where heaves the turf in many a mouldering heap,
15 Each in his narrow cell for ever laid,
16 The rude forefathers of the hamlet sleep.

17 The breezy call of incense-breathing morn,
18 The swallow twittering from the straw-built shed,
19 The cock's shrill clarion, or the echoing horn,
20 No more shall rouse them from their lowly bed.

21 For them no more the blazing hearth shall burn,
22 Or busy housewife ply her evening care:
23 No children run to lisp their sire's return,
24 Or climb his knees the envied kiss to share.

25 Oft did the harvest to their sickle yield,
26 Their furrow oft the stubborn glebe has broke;
27 How jocund did they drive their team afield!
28 How bowed the woods beneath their sturdy stroke!

29 Let not Ambition mock their useful toil,
30 Their homely joys, and destiny obscure;
31 Nor Grandeur hear with a disdainful smile,
32 The short and simple annals of the poor.

33 The boast of heraldry, the pomp of power,
34 And all that beauty, all that wealth e'er gave,
35 Awaits alike the inevitable hour.
36 The paths of glory lead but to the grave.

37 Nor you, ye Proud, impute to these the fault,
38 If Memory o'er their tomb no trophies raise,
39 Where through the long-drawn aisle and fretted vault
40 The pealing anthem swells the note of praise.

41 Can storied urn or animated bust
42 Back to its mansion call the fleeting breath?
43 Can Honour's voice provoke the silent dust,
44 Or Flattery soothe the dull cold ear of Death?

45 Perhaps in this neglected spot is laid
46 Some heart once pregnant with celestial fire;
47 Hands that the rod of empire might have swayed,
48 Or waked to ecstasy the living lyre.

49   But Knowledge to their eyes her ample page
50   Rich with the spoils of time did ne'er unroll;
51   Chill Penury repressed their noble rage,
52   And froze the genial current of the soul.

53   Full many a gem of purest ray serene,
54   The dark unfathomed caves of ocean bear:
55   Full many a flower is born to blush unseen,
56   And waste its sweetness on the desert air.

57   Some village-Hampden, that with dauntless breast
58   The little tyrant of his fields withstood;
59   Some mute inglorious Milton here may rest,
60   Some Cromwell guiltless of his country's blood.

61   The applause of listening senates to command,
62   The threats of pain and ruin to despise,
63   To scatter plenty o'er a smiling land,
64   And read their history in a nation's eyes,

65   Their lot forbade: nor circumscribed alone
66   Their growing virtues, but their crimes confined;
67   Forbade to wade through slaughter to a throne,
68   And shut the gates of mercy on mankind,

69   The struggling pangs of conscious truth to hide,
70   To quench the blushes of ingenuous shame,
71   Or heap the shrine of Luxury and Pride
72   With incense kindled at the Muse's flame.

73   Far from the madding crowd's ignoble strife,
74   Their sober wishes never learned to stray;
75   Along the cool sequestered vale of life
76   They kept the noiseless tenor of their way.

77   Yet even these bones from insult to protect
78   Some frail memorial still erected nigh,
79   With uncouth rhymes and shapeless sculpture decked,
80   Implores the passing tribute of a sigh.

81   Their name, their years, spelt by the unlettered muse,
82   The place of fame and elegy supply:
83   And many a holy text around she strews,
84   That teach the rustic moralist to die.

85   For who to dumb Forgetfulness a prey,
86   This pleasing anxious being e'er resigned,
87   Left the warm precincts of the cheerful day,
88   Nor cast one longing lingering look behind?

89   On some fond breast the parting soul relies,
90   Some pious drops the closing eye requires;
91   Ev'n from the tomb the voice of nature cries,
92   Ev'n in our ashes live their wonted fires.

93   For thee, who mindful of the unhonoured dead
94   Dost in these lines their artless tale relate;
95   If chance, by lonely Contemplation led,
96   Some kindred spirit shall inquire thy fate,

97   Haply some hoary-headed swain may say,
98   'Oft have we seen him at the peep of dawn
99   'Brushing with hasty steps the dews away
100 'To meet the sun upon the upland lawn.

101 'There at the foot of yonder nodding beech
102 'That wreathes its old fantastic roots so high,
103 'His listless length at noontide would he stretch,
104 'And pore upon the brook that babbles by.

105 'Hard by yon wood, now smiling as in scorn,
106 'Muttering his wayward fancies he would rove,
107 'Now drooping, woeful wan, like one forlorn,
108 'Or crazed with care, or crossed in hopeless love.

109 'One morn I missed him on the customed hill,
110 'Along the heath and near his favourite tree;
111 'Another came; nor yet beside the rill,
112 'Nor up the lawn, nor at the wood was he;

113 'The next with dirges due in sad array
114 'Slow through the church-way path we saw him borne.
115 'Approach and read (for thou can'st read) the lay,
116 'Graved on the stone beneath yon aged thorn.'

The Epitaph

117 Here rests his head upon the lap of earth
118 A youth to fortune and to fame unknown.
119 Fair Science frowned not on his humble birth,
120 And Melancholy marked him for her own.

121 Large was his bounty, and his soul sincere,
122 Heaven did a recompense as largely send:
123 He gave to Misery all he had, a tear,
124 He gained from Heaven ('twas all he wished) a friend.

125 No farther seek his merits to disclose,
126 Or draw his frailties from their dread abode,
127 (There they alike in trembling hope repose)
128 The bosom of his Father and his God.

Subject: Diana's Detour 263
Fri, Aug 8, 2014

How many funerals end with everyone singing, "All you need is love" by the Beatles?

And "What a wonderful world" sung by Louis Armstrong (1901 – 1971)?

"What A Wonderful World"[66]
George David Weiss/Bob Thiele

I see trees of green,
red roses too.
I see them bloom,
for me and you.
And I think to myself,
what a wonderful world.

I see skies of blue,
And clouds of white.
The bright blessed day,
The dark sacred night.
And I think to myself,
What a wonderful world.

The colors of the rainbow,
So pretty in the sky.
Are also on the faces,
Of people going by,
I see friends shaking hands.
Saying, "How do you do?"
They're really saying,
"I love you".

I hear babies cry,
I watch them grow,
They'll learn much more,
Than I'll ever know.
And I think to myself,
What a wonderful world.

Yes, I think to myself,
What a wonderful world.

Oh yeah.

Subject: Diana's Detour 264
Sat, Aug 9, 2014

In my own judgmental, narrow-minded,
limited-to-my-own-experience-of-the-world kind of way,
I assumed
(and never assume anything, because it just "makes an 'ass'
out of 'u' and 'me'")
that my friend who recently died was a musician, yes,
and washed windows for a living, yes,
but that it was his wife who was principal source of support
for their family.

I could not have been more wrong.
I learned at his memorial service that he was a successful
entrepreneur who had spun off 10 window-washing
franchises, and made a very good salary.
He built a business model that started in Colorado and
allowed him to earn enough money so that he could spend

more time doing what he loved ~ be with his family and make music.

CNN even did a feature on him in 1999.

And I know him only as that sweet guy with a very positive attitude who put together Christmas caroling in Takoma Park.

I've always thought that the best kind of philanthropy was the kind that provided employment opportunities for people.

And that's exactly what he did.

Someone at his funeral referred to it as his "ministry."

Subject: Diana's Detour 265
Sunday, Aug 10, 2014

On this, the night of the Super Moon.

Pat Conroy (1945-2016)[67]
The Prince of Tides

"One bright summer night, when we were very small and the humid air hung like moss over the low country, my sister and brother and I could not sleep. Our mother took us out of the house, Savannah and I with summer colds, and Luke with a heat rash, and walked all of us down to the river and out onto the dock.

"I have a surprise for you, my darlings," our mother said as we watched a porpoise move toward the Atlantic through the still, metallic waters. We sat at the end of the floating dock and stretched our legs, trying to touch the water with our bare feet.

"There's something I want you to see, something that will help you sleep. Look over there, children," she said, pointing out toward the horizon to the east.

It was growing dark on this long summer evening and suddenly, at the exact point her finger had indicated, the moon lifted a forehead of stunning gold above the horizon, lifted straight out of filigree, light-intoxicated clouds that lay on the skyline in attendant veils. Behind us, the sun was setting in a simultaneous congruent withdrawal and the river turned to flame in a quiet duel of gold … The new gold of moon astonishing and ascendant, the depleted gold of sunset extinguishing itself in the long westward slide, it was the old dance of days in the Carolina marshes, the breathtaking death of days before the eyes of children, until the sun vanished, its final signature a ribbon of bullion strung across the tops of water oaks. The moon then rose quickly, rose like a bird from the water, from the trees, from the islands, and climbed straight up – gold, then yellow, then pale yellow, pale silver, silver-bright, then something miraculous, immaculate, and beyond silver, a color native o only to Southern nights.

We children sat transfixed before that moon our mother had called forth from the waters. When the moon had reached its deepest silver, my sister, Savannah, though only three, cried aloud to our mother, to Luke and me, to the river and the moon, "Oh, Mama, do it again!" And I had my earliest memory.""

Ever since I read this passage many years ago, I had wanted to be able to do that.
To be with children near the water at sunset.
To watch the sun go down, and then the moon rise
As if exchanging one for the other.

Subject: Re: Diana's Detour 266
Mon, Aug 11, 2014

So much to do.
So little time before blast-off on Thursday afternoon.

Just found out my cousin may have a granddaughter born while we are in Lithuania.

So many people to see there.
So little time.

And now I have promised to write an article about my WWI diarist. Visit to her area Aug 20.

Aug 23rd marks the 25th anniversary of The Baltic Way, when 2 million Estonians, Latvians and Lithuanians held hands and formed a human chain spanning over 370 miles across three countries in protest of 50 years of Soviet occupation. There is bound to be some re-enactment or commemoration while we are there.

So much history to absorb.
And so many places to visit.

8/18	Vilnius
8/19	Vilnius, Trakai, Gruto Parkas
8/20	Panevėžys, Puziniškis, Joniškėlis
8/21	Kryžiu Kalnas, Šauliai, Kuršėnai, Palanga, Nida
8/22	Klaipėda, Marijampolė
8/23	Marijampolė, Kalvarija,
8/24	Marijampolė, Kazlų Rūda
8/25	Kaunas, Vilnius
8/26	Vilnius

I am renting a car for the part outside Vilnius. Do I need an international drivers license?

Subject: Diana's Detour 267
Tue, Aug 12, 2014

Soft summer rain, which we very much needed.
No wind, just wet and misty.
Pretty dark at noon, cars driving with lights on.

We got an inch or two, but Baltimore was hit with 8 inches.
They even closed the harbor tunnel for a while.

Should I take a giant umbrella with me to the land of rain?
Because I love walking under one.
But with so much to keep track of while traveling,
I'm bound to leave it somewhere.

I understand the record-setting heat wave has broken in Lithuania.
Just in time for us to continue in fall weather mode.

My last day of work before vacation is tomorrow, Wednesday,
and my flight departs at 5pm Thursday.

Then I will enter the world of cobblestones and multiple centuries of architecture.
I like that, according to Wikipedia:

"Vilnius has some of the highest Internet speeds in the world, with an average download speed of 36.37 MB/s and upload speed of 28.51 MB/s...

Vilnius has access to groundwater, and there is no need to use extensive chemicals in treating surface water from lakes or rivers, providing residents with some of the cleanest and healthiest tap water access in Europe."

Subject: Diana's Detour 268
Wed, Aug 13, 2014

A chocolate croissant for breakfast.
A job in a nice office to go to.
A Greek salad for lunch.
Sometimes enjoyed on the sunny roof of that downtown office.
A modest brick house, walking distance from the subway, to come home to.
Two nice girls renting rooms in my house.
Kitty will be well taken care of in my absence.

Need to buy bubble wrap before I can finish packing.
I think Kinko's opens early.

The nighttime air is jingling with cicada song.
My son complained about the loudness when he was visiting from San Francisco last week.
Many years ago, a cousin visiting from Lithuania stuck a tape recorder out her window and recorded it.
She said it sounded like a jungle out there.

Subject: Diana's Detour 269
Thur, Aug 14, 2014

Copenhagen airport.
You literally have to walk through stores to get to your plane.
H&M open for shopping at 7am.
Gucci and Burberry, too.
Thumping music throughout.
Everyone very chic in black, white, or grey.

I like that Norwegian airlines has the picture of a Swedish poet, Evert Taube, featured on the tail of one of its planes.

Subject: Re: Diana's Detour 270
Fri, Aug 15, 2014

"You look like Annie Lenox of the Eurythmics with that hair! People will be asking for your autograph!"

So, for the first time, I went public wigless, and it was in Vilnius.
No one asked for my autograph, but it still felt good.

It's Žolinės in Lithuania today, a national holiday celebrating pre-Christian traditions linked with completing the most important farming chores, as summer merges into autumn. The Catholic Church made it the Feast of the Assumption, the taking up of the Blessed Virgin Mary's body into Heaven.

The oversized mason jars that I had thickly bubble-wrapped for my cousin's kiosk business arrived unbroken!
And we all enjoyed the chocolate-covered bacon I had brought in from the Amish market in Laurel, Maryland.

We walked and walked all over Old Town Vilnius this evening. It stays light until about 10pm. A perfect night. Sidewalk cafes full. The city oozes history.

A wonderful little old man in the Uniate Church near the Gates of Dawn explained in no uncertain terms how much destruction had been wreaked upon churches during the Soviet era. They are proudly displaying support of Ukraine.

Subject: Diana's Detour 271
Saturday, Aug 16, 2014

"Is that you?"
Ran into my first Lithuanian-Americans in Vilnius, a couple I used to know from San Diego.
They spend their summers in their apartment in Užupis, a part of Vilnius "on the other side of the river" that has declared itself a separate republic. Here is its constitution:[68]

1. *Everyone has the right to live by the River Vilnelė, and the River Vilnelė has the right to flow by everyone.*
2. *Everyone has the right to hot water, heating in winter and a tiled roof.*
3. *Everyone has the right to die, but this is not an obligation.*
4. *Everyone has the right to make mistakes.*
5. *Everyone has the right to be unique.*

6. *Everyone has the right to love.*
7. *Everyone has the right not to be loved, but not necessarily.*
8. *Everyone has the right to be undistinguished and unknown.*
9. *Everyone has the right to be idle.*
10. *Everyone has the right to love and take care of a cat.*
11. *Everyone has the right to look after the dog until one of them dies.*
12. *A dog has the right to be a dog.*
13. *A cat is not obliged to love its owner, but must help in time of need.*
14. *Sometimes everyone has the right to be unaware of their duties.*
15. *Everyone has the right to be in doubt, but this is not an obligation.*
16. *Everyone has the right to be happy.*
17. *Everyone has the right to be unhappy.*
18. *Everyone has the right to be silent.*
19. *Everyone has the right to have faith.*
20. *No one has the right to violence.*
21. *Everyone has the right to appreciate their unimportance.*
22. *No one has the right to have a design on eternity.*
23. *Everyone has the right to understand.*
24. *Everyone has the right to understand nothing.*
25. *Everyone has the right to be of any nationality.*
26. *Everyone has the right to celebrate or not celebrate their birthday.*
27. *Everyone shall remember their name.*
28. *Everyone may share what they possess.*
29. *No one can share what they do not possess.*
30. *Everyone has the right to have brothers, sisters and parents.*

31. *Everyone may be independent.*
32. *Everyone is responsible for their freedom.*
33. *Everyone has the right to cry.*
34. *Everyone has the right to be misunderstood.*
35. *No one has the right to make another person guilty.*
36. *Everyone has the right to be individual.*
37. *Everyone has the right to have no rights.*
38. *Everyone has the right to not to be afraid.*
39. *Do not defeat*
40. *Do not fight back*
41. *Do not surrender*

Subject: Diana's Detour 272
Sun, Aug 17, 2014

Since arriving Friday evening, I have met with
—my wonderful cousin Nomeda and her husband and her mother
—my children's first nanny, who also happens to be a famous rheumatologist, and her family
—one of my exchange scientists (a biochemist) from 30 years ago and his family
—the couple from San Diego

A new Bieliauskas (or rather "Bieliauskaitė" as the mark of the unwed female) has been born: Jonė.

And this was just a precursor to my daughter's flying in tonight from San Francisco via Copenhagen
And her boyfriend's flying in tonight from Los Angeles via Moscow.
Hospitality required an arrival dinner at midnight.
Now the adventure begins...

Subject: Diana's Detour 273
Mon, Aug 18, 2014

I have got to stop having this much fun.
Another beautiful sweater-weather day in sunny Vilnius!
Exploring the winding mini-streets of old town
Navigating the cobblestones
Peeking into courtyards of parked automobiles, hanging wash, and blooming flowers.

Got a tour of the Jewish sites of Vilnius
Which is basically much of old town
With someone who survived the Holocaust.

We walk the same stones as people have for hundreds of years.
Napoleon did.
These streets were lined with the frozen bodies of French soldiers
After their retreat from Moscow.

Now it's outdoor cafe after outdoor cafe.
Interestingly, not a Russian word in sight.

Subject: Diana's Detour 274
Tues, Aug 19, 2014

Blue skies and 66 lakes, verdant islands, an orange castle.
Eight of us went sailing around Trakai this afternoon.

On the boat, we snacked on "kibinai" which looked and tasted remarkably like the Jamaican meat patties we enjoy back in Maryland. These pastries, however, are a tradition of the Karaim or Turkish Jews who migrated to Eastern Europe from Crimea in the 13th century.

The train out was brand new and comfortable,
The bus back the same.

A half hour from bustling Vilnius, we are in a 14th century island world.
Where all is peaceful.

No one I talk to in Vilnius really feels that Putin would attack them.
Yes, it would be a good idea to be prepared, but ...

I keep thinking of how the Berlin Wall was thrown up while the Kennedys were vacationing in Hyannisport in 1961.
Bad things happen in late August.

Just think of this weekend, August 23, 1939.
The Molotov-Ribbentrop Agreement that unleashed WWII 75 years ago.

The new Putin doctrine seems to be, let's Europe and Russia be friends
And let those crazy Americans enjoy their phobia.

Subject: Diana's Detour 275
Wed, Aug 20, 2014

What an idiot.
When it came time to buy gas for our rented car, I kept shoving my credit card into the slot with the blinking lights.

Two times it went in, was rejected, and got spit out.
The third time, the machine kept trying to eject my card, but was obviously stuck.
That's when I realized I had inserted my credit card into the slot intended for cash.

Despite all the clear instructions on the machine, including colored pictures of Lithuanian bills in one spot and a credit card in another
This American still went for the blinking lights and stuck her card in where it did not belong.

So here I am, part of a motorcade from the Panevėžys library, heading to a museum at a far away site that they have opened especially for our visit.

And this, a fully automated gas station, with no attendant.

In an impressive display of efficiency, the help number on the machine worked, and in less than half an hour, my card was rescued and we were on our way.

In the meantime, everyone in the entourage was in high spirits, my fellow customers encouraging and good natured, and the ladies from the library insisting that the author who is the object of my obsession would not have allowed me to be upset.

Not even almost running over a pine tree on the 15-kilometer gravel road back from the site could stop us from laughing.

We are finally at Palanga on the Baltic Sea.

It has gotten windy and rainy, but the stormy views driving across this very flat part of Lithuania called "Žemaitija" were spectacular.

Flat can be good.

Subject: Diana's Detour 276
Thursday, Aug 21, 2014

I am in heaven.
The place we booked in the lovely bayside resort of Nida really is a fisherman's hut!
Right on the main drag, with a high-rise hotel next door and a Wal-Mart sized "Maxima" behind it.
We are in a picturesque wooden house surrounded by a cottage garden.
And the proprietor is a lovely woman in her forties who lives on site,
Has a loom set up outside to weave rugs.
Cooks outside and has a whole kitchen arranged there under a canopy
During the tourist season sleeps in a comfortable shed.
Moves back into this totally remodeled fisherman's hut for the winter.
I want her life.

We climbed the wooden steps up to the majestic dunes late this afternoon
From where you literally can see Russia (Kaliningrad)
And then wandered atop them
Sat on the sand to drink in the quiet and the views.
While the wind whipped around us.

Once a German painters' retreat
Then a private holiday region for Nazi officers
Later reserved for Communist party officials
Nida remains charming
And we are so happy to be here.

**Subject: Diana's Detour 277 and 277
Saturday, Aug 23, 2014**

I love, love, love our cousins in Lithuania.
It made the 4 1/2 hour drive from the seaside to Marijampolė totally worth it
to see them all gathered in the back yard as we pulled in

From a family of four brothers, three were there with their wives, all of whom are wonderful.
I learned that practically all of us have had cancer,
and one cousin's wife had been operated on for the same cancer at practically the same time that I was
So we both missed last October's gathering.

But before even getting to Marijampolė, we stopped in Kalvarija to visit my late father's last living sibling
And my cousin who cares for her.
Who prepared for us the first of many feasts.
That all seem to include a Greek salad
And baked a hundred-leaf cake for us, her specialty.

I am being loaded down with honey.
I didn't even mention our stop in Kuršėnai en route to the seaside.
To see my mother's relatives.

So many are, although nobody speaks of it, survivors of
Siberia.
Many of them were exiled as children
As "enemies of the Soviet state"
And shunned upon their return
The population cowed in perpetual fear.

And they are the most generous.
Four jars of honey.

That bubble wrap should come in handy.

Subject: Diana's Detour 279
Sunday, Aug 24, 2014

We drove back to Vilnius in the pouring rain today
And it has been raining nonstop ever since.
The raindrops pounding the metal dormers
In this mediaeval city
But muffled to silence on the clay tiled roofs.

The next generation of cousins
Those with school-aged children
Who live in the smaller towns
Have all built magnificent modern homes
And have beautifully landscaped yards
Planted with apple and pear trees
Greenhouses
Gardens
Compost quarters
The moms look like models
They vacation in Austria or the Tenerifes (Canary Islands).

And everybody has a full time job.

The cousin we're staying with in old town Vilnius
Never wanted the bother of a house.
She'd rather read a book
Soak in art, plays, concerts
And revel in the stone city that's been hers since childhood.

Subject: Diana's Detour 280
Monday, Aug 25, 2014

Cold, cold, cold.
It's about 50 degrees here now.
Spells of rain and sun, off and on.
But no rainbows.

Enjoyed a lovely three-hour lunch with friends from Silver
Spring who moved here 10 years ago.
In their mid-60s, with a three-floor apartment to die for.
They are happy academics who enjoy concerts, art galleries,
and other performing arts
All within walking distance
In a picturesque European setting.

When I visited the back lot at Warner Brothers in California,
the European section looked just like the streets of Vilnius.

I must admit, I am getting a little tired of walking on
cobblestones.
The streets are narrow, the sidewalks even more so, and
unchanged for hundreds of years.

I can only imagine wide carriages careening down these lanes and people hugging the sides of buildings to keep from being run over.

Lithuanians are a very patient sort. Docile. Attentive.
Went to an outdoor concert tonight.
By a popular young classical accordionist who looks like Benedict Cumberbatch
He usually plays Beethoven to Vivaldi, but tonight tried something experimental.
Atonal. Cacophonic. The audience was rapt.

Subject: Diana's Detour 281
Tues, Aug 26, 2014

No, no, no waved the guard.
No selfies by the seal of the American Embassy.
He pointed to a picture of a camera with a line struck through it.
I hadn't noticed it, of course.

On this trip, in addition to totally not seeing signs forbidding photos,
misplacing my car keys right as the ferry is unloading,
And sticking my credit card into a slot meant for cash,
I have forgotten to take my cell phone places,
Misplaced my electric power adapter
Brought the wrong gifts

My daughter pleaded with me to reassure her that I was always this way
And that it was not a condition she should expect to grow into.

I assured her that I was.

Tonight is their last night, and they fly out in 7 hours.
I have one more day.
Hard to believe, as I feel so at home here.
But I'm sure I've gained 10 pounds....
I blame those garlic-sprinkled fried rye-bread chips.

Subject: Re: Diana's Detour 282
Wed, Aug 27, 2014

Ferns, moss, and forest floor.
So glad we decided to go mushrooming for my last day in
Lithuania.

Another quiet, watchful activity, taking place in a natural
setting.
Sunny but autumn like. We had to bundle up and wear
boots.

I believe this is a country of introverts
Where everyone gets recharged by being alone, outdoors,
but doing something vaguely in a group.

Finding mushrooms requires a lot of concentration and feels
like detective work.
They're hiding in plain sight, just camouflaged.

Unlike walking a labyrinth to let the thoughts in your mind
unwind
You're focusing on the area at your feet to see what might
be concealed.

The "aha" moment comes when a tuft of leaves looks just a little too high
And underneath can be anything from yummy boletus to poisonous Cortinarius orellanus.

Then the process of sorting and cleaning and cutting up the various types of mushrooms we'd picked
Reminded me a lot of the mess entailed in eating Maryland crab.

It's a great conversation activity
But don't expect to eat soon.

I can't get enough of the beautiful old wooden houses we pass in the countryside,
with the filigreed gables and shutters
the glass-paned porches
the impressively deep window sills
the massive ovens, with their sleeping benches.

Last minute shopping for graphics, linen kitchen towels, some amber, some chocolate, some cheese.

My flight leaves in six hours.
Good night.

Subject: Diana's Detour 283
Thurs, Aug 28, 2014

"Your bag is overweight; for the extra charge of....."
I quickly emptied my bag of four large jars of homemade
honey.
Still thickly bubble wrapped.
"Can I give these to anyone?" I asked
"You can give them to us!"

At 6 am in the Vilnius airport, I was glad that local rules
allowed my honey to be re-gifted, rather than landfilled.

"And what can I do with this heavy (coffee table) book
about Panevėžys?"
"Oh, I'm from Panevėžys!"

Turns out, the ticket clerk who volunteered to take the
honey was not only from Panevėžys
but she also knew all about the object of my literary
obsession,
Gabrielė Petkevičaitė-Bitė
had even lived in her house on St. Zita Street,
that I believe my mother lived in when she was 10 year old
and the agent's father used to work there.

Sometimes I feel like a cult within a cult.

Subject: Diana's Detour 284
Friday, Aug 29, 2014

My left foot searches for a clutch
While my right hand keeps fumbling for gears that aren't
there..
Ah, the relearned behaviors from driving a stick shift
Have now to be unlearned.

Much as I would love to imagine myself living in a
fisherman's shack in Nida,
or in one of the picturesque old houses on a farm In
Lithuania
I think I would get bored with my own company pretty fast
No matter how exotic and inspiring the setting.

If only I were an artist.
As a couple of my relatives are turning out to be in their
later years.
One took up oil painting.
Another paints beautifully on silk scarves.

The outdoors are ringing now with the song of cicadas
All night long

So parched and hot back here in Maryland.
I had a lot of watering to do.
Mowed the grass.
Got new front brakes on the car.
Defrosted the refrigerator as the freezer door had frozen
shut.
Cleaned house in anticipation of my nephew's and niece's
arriving tonight.

So glad to have a day off from work after returning from my trip.
So sorry to be missing a wedding in Boston.
But I really was not sure I could make the drive safely while jetlagged
Despite having arranged to return in time for it.

Subject: Diana's Detour 285
Sat, Aug 30, 2014

Coal capsules.
That's right, black capsules containing coal.
That's what I was given when my stomach acted up in Lithuania
From the strong coffee
And they worked like magic!

I am told one can get them at health food stores in the US.
What with my egg whites cure for burning hands,
and coal for an upset stomach
I feel like I've stumbled back in time

I definitely feel like I've stumbled back from autumn into summer.

Bought a bunch of "steppable" plants at the nursery today
To try to approximate the beautiful yards I saw in Lithuania.
Will have to put them in damp areas of my yard
Set them off, not bunch them together
And really build up the soil.

I thought our earth was pretty good here,
But it is really dark and loamy and beautiful where my relatives live.

Subject: Diana's Detour 286
Sun, Aug 31, 2014

Sometimes when there is nothing but bad news in the world,
One just wants to retreat and tend one's garden.

In the words of Voltaire:

During this conversation, news was spread abroad that two viziers of the bench and the mufti had just been strangled at Constantinople, and several of their friends empaled. This catastrophe made a great noise for some hours. Pangloss, Candide, and Martin, as they were returning to the little farm, met with a good-looking old man, who was taking the air at his door, under an alcove formed of the boughs of orange-trees. Pangloss, who was as inquisitive as he was disputative, asked him what was the name of the mufti who was lately strangled. "I cannot tell," answered the good old man; "I never knew the name of any mufti, or vizier breathing. I am entirely ignorant of the event you speak of; I presume that in general such as are concerned in public affairs sometimes come to a miserable end; and that they deserve it: but I never inquire what is doing at Constantinople; I am contented with sending thither the produce of my garden, which I cultivate with my own hands." After saying these words, he invited the strangers to come into his house. His two daughters and two sons presented them with divers sorts of sherbet of their own making; besides caymac, heightened with the peels of candied citrons, oranges, lemons, pineapples, pistachio nuts, and Mocha coffee unadulterated with the bad coffee of Batavia or the American islands. After which the two daughters of this good Mussulman perfumed the beards of Candide, Pangloss, and Martin.

Subject: Diana's Detour 287
Mon, Sep 1, 2014
Labor Day

Yesterday's post was about this:

After his long journey across Europe and Asia Minor, Voltaire has his hero Candide settle down on the outskirts of the Muslim city of Constantinople to "tend his own garden," in other words "to mind his own business." After witnessing horrifying episodes of religious intolerance and political oppression, Candide decides that the best thing to do in the world is settle down, live peacefully with his neighbours, and produce something of value to others which he can sell in the markets.

Friends of mine have just returned from Constantinople/Istanbul/Byzantium.
The people there were so kind, they said.
Just as we experienced in Egypt.
A kindness that is part of their very being, of their culture.
They say American soldiers in Iraq had to teach their trainees how to yell.
It was not part of their nature.

Many people are citing W.H. Auden's poem, September 1, 1939 today.
Written on the occasion of the outbreak of WWII.

It is now exactly a century since the outbreak of WWI.
75 years since the outbreak of WWII.
And the winds of war seem swirling about us again.

Subject: Diana's Detour 288
Tues, Sep 2, 2014

First day back at work at 9:00 am.
First day back at boot camp before that at 5:30 am.
I feel energized but a little sleep-deprived.

Labor Day weekend is also the anniversary of my cancer
showing itself.
I carried on with boot camp for a few more weeks, but then
had to quit.

It's great to be back.
"You've kept your core strong" remarked my trainer.
That's thanks to her.

Who knew how important your stomach muscles would
prove in recovery?
When you've got to pull yourself out of bed to hobble to the
bathroom while dragging along a pole with all sorts of IVs
and tubes.
You have to unplug everything from the wall each time,
because it's pumping fluids into you, not just dripping
them.
Then re-attach.
Lots of twisting and turning.

But I'm too sore from the sumo squat jumps to the 20-yard
line to exercise tomorrow.
Have to give this body a rest.

Subject: Diana's Detour 289
Wed, Sep 3, 2014

Ten years have passed. And now this.

August 31, 2004
In the Absence of Sparrows[69]
Daniel Johnson

Rockets concuss. Guns rattle off.
Dogs in a public square
feed on dead horses.

I don't know, Jim, where you are.
When did you last see
birds? The winter sky in Boston

is gray with flu. Newspapers,
senators, friends, even your mom
on Good Morning America—

no one knows where you are.
It's night, cold and bruised,
where you are. Plastic twine binds

your hands. You wait and pray, pray
and wait, but this is where the picture goes gray.
We don't know, Jim, where you are.

*

In the absence of sparrows: a crowd of friends and family gather in
*   Rochester,*
New Hampshire to recite the holy rosary.

*

We keep your picture on the kitchen table, pack of American Spirits,
airplane bottle of Scotch, a copy of Krapp's Last Tape.

Don't get me wrong; we expect you back. Skinny, feral,
coffee eyes sunken but alive, you've always come back, from Iraq,

Syria, Afghanistan, even Libya after Gaddafi's forces
captured and held you for 44 days. You tracked time scratching

marks with your zipper on prison walls, scrawling notes on cigarette
boxes, reciting the Koran with other prisoners. Then, you called.

DJ, it's Jimmy…I'm in New Hampshire, brother! I wanted
to break your f—-ing nose. We ate lobster rolls, instead,

on a picnic bench by Boston Harbor. You made a quick round
of TV shows, packed your camera and Arabic phrasebook.

You skipped town on a plane to Turkey. We talked once. You said
you'd play it safe. The connection was lost.

*

In the absence of sparrows: American journalist James Foley
        disappeared
after being taken captive by armed gunmen near Aleppo, Syria on
        Thanksgiving Day.

In the absence of sparrows: our house burns blue with news.

*

Winter solstice, 1991. You turned donuts,
drinking beers, in a snowy public lot next to the lake.
Girls yelped. You cranked the Pixies louder, cut the lights,
and steered Billy's grandma's Chrysler onto the Winnipesaukee ice.
The moon flamed bright as a county coroner's light.
You revved the station wagon's engine. Billy tied
a yellow ski rope off the hitch, flashed a thumbs up,
and you punched the gas — 5, 15, 20, 25 miles per hour —
towing Billy, skating in high-top sneakers,
across the frozen lake. Chill air filled his lungs.
Billy pumped his fist. You torqued the wheel left.
Triumphant, you honked and flashed the lights.
You took a swig of Heineken and wheeled
the wood-paneled station wagon in a wide-arcing turn
to pick up Billy, bloodied but standing. People do reckless things
but your friends dubbed you the High King of Foolish S — t.
The nose of Billy's grandma's Chrysler broke the ice.
You jammed it into reverse. Bald tires spinning,
you flung yourself from the car. In seconds, it was gone.
You gave Billy's grandma a potted mum
and a silver balloon. Standing on her screened-in porch,
you mumbled an apology. What am I supposed to do now?
she asked. What the hell do I do now?

*

In the absence of sparrows: when falling snow, out the window,
    looks like radio waves,
  your face appears, your baritone laugh.

We read Abbie Hoffman, 1968, watched Panther documentaries,
The Weather Underground, and packed our bandanas, first aid kits,
fat markers, maps and signs for New York City. A31, they called it,
a day of direct action, a time to heave ourselves on the gears

of an odious machine. We marched, drumming and chanting, half
a million strong,
through the streets of Lower Manhattan. Worst President Ever, A
Texas Village
Has Lost Its Idiot. Protestors carried a flotilla of flag-covered coffins.
We hoisted homemade signs and cried out, Whose streets?
Our streets? No justice, no peace! I'd packed sandwiches,
water, mapped restrooms along the parade route, inked
the hotline for Legal Services on your forearm and mine.
You, my wild half brother, packed only a one hitter, notepad, and pen.
When the parade snaked past the New York Public Library,
we peeled off to confront 20 cops in riot gear blocking entry
with batons drawn. We took position on the library steps.
Stone-still, inches from police, we held our signs
stamped with a student gagged by padlock and chain.
I could feel breath on my neck. We narrowly escaped arrest,
then streamed toward the Garden, a ragtag troop of 200.
We evaded barricades. Cut down alleys. At Herald Square, only
blocks from the Republican Convention, cops on mopeds
cut us off. They rolled out a bright orange snow fence,
hundreds of yard long, then zip cuffed us, one by one.
I called Ebele. You called your brother, set to be married in just three
days.
His best man, you were headed to jail. "I'll be there Friday for the golf
outing,"
you vowed, a cop cutting your phone call short. They took you first.
Threw you on a city bus headed to Pier 14 on the Hudson,
a giant garage stinking of axel grease and gasoline. Stepping off the
bus,
I scanned hundreds of faces staring through chain link, newly erected
and topped with concertina wire. I couldn't find you. I can't. They
transferred me,
in soapy light, to the Tombs, Manhattan's city jail, and freed me
after 24 hours
to wander the streets. I peered in Chinese restaurants, seedy Canal

Street bars,
called your cell phone from a payphone, trekked to Yago's apartment
in Spanish Harlem, eager to crack beers, to begin weaving the story
we would always tell. You were not there. Waiting outside the Tombs,
I missed my flight home. Waiting, I smoked your cigarettes on the fire
escape.
They held you and held you. You are missing still. I want to hold you.
Beauty
is in the streets, my brother. Beauty is in the streets.
*

In the absence of sparrows: trash fires, a call to prayer. Dusk.
Rockets whistling, plastic bags taking flight.
In the absence of sparrows: all of a sudden, you appear. Standing
before a cinder block
wall, you're holding a video camera with a boom mic and wearing a
bulletproof
vest.
In the absence of sparrows: the front page story says you've been
missing since
November 22, 2012. Everything else it doesn't say.
In the absence of sparrows: you simply wandered off, past the Sunoco,
pockets stuffed.
The door to your apartment is open still —

James Wright "Jim" Foley (October 18, 1973 – c. August 19, 2014) was an American journalist and video reporter. While working as a freelance war correspondent during the Syrian Civil War, he was abducted on November 22, 2012, in northwestern Syria. He was beheaded in August 2014 as a response to American airstrikes in Iraq, thus becoming the first American citizen killed by the Islamic State of Iraq and the Levant (ISIL, ISIS, Islamic State, IS).

Subject: Diana's Detour 290
Thurs, Sep 4, 2014

Some of us will remember this song:

"Try to remember the kind of September
When life was slow and oh so mellow
Try to remember the kind of September
When grass was green and grain so yellow
Try to remember the kind of September
When you were a young and a callow fellow
Try to remember and if you remember
Then follow—follow, oh-oh."

- "Try to Remember," Lyrics by Tom Jones and Harvey Schmidt[70]

Subject: Diana's 291
Fri, Sep 5, 2014

"Lyric night of the lingering Indian Summer,
Shadowy fields that are scentless but full of singing,
Never a bird, but the passionless chant of insects,
Ceaseless, insistent.
The grasshopper's horn, and far-off, high in the maples,
The wheel of a locust leisurely grinding the silence
Under a moon waning and worn, broken,
Tired with summer."

Sarah Teasdale (1884-1933)
September Midnights[71]

Subject: Diana's Detour 292
Saturday, Sep 6, 2014

"The true beloveds of this world are in their lover's eyes lilacs opening, ship lights, school bells, a landscape, remembered conversations, friends, a child's Sunday, lost voices, one's favorite suit, autumn and all seasons, memory, yes, it being the earth and water of existence, memory."

Truman Capote (1924-1984)
Other Voices, Other Rooms (1948)[72]

Subject: Diana's Detour 293
Sun, Sep 7, 2014

What a crushing rain last night.
After a crushingly hot day.
And what a beautifully fresh, cool autumn Sunday greeted me as I opened the front door this morning.

The annual Takoma Park Folk Festival is enjoying good attendance
judging from all the people walking past my house to the middle school.

I must be that woman working in her front yard whom passersby feel comfortable chatting up.
Like I'm part of the local scenery, a "native informant..."

One couple asked about the Celosia I have growing on my sidewalk terrace.

I believe it's Celosia argentea var. spicata (Pink Flamingo Feather Flower).
Might also be Celosia Caracas, Celosia wheatstraw

I read that it is known in Africa as Lagos spinach. *"Harvested before it flowers, the plant is an important leaf vegetable in tropical Africa and Southeast Asia. In Nigeria, it is called soko yokoto, which means 'make husbands fat and happy.' In Swahili, it's called mfungu."*
All part of the amaranth family.

I love Celosia cockscomb for the fall, although I haven't seen much of it around this year.
Usually, Mrs. K's Toll House, an old restaurant a few miles away, is red-velveted in cockscombs in the autumn.
Just not this year.

And this Celosia was different
I bought it because it had floppy, almost worm-like blossoms that were covered with bees.
The bees still love them.

"Autumn is a second spring when every leaf is a flower."
Albert Camus (1913-1960)[73]

Subject: Diana's Detour 294
Mon, Sep 8, 2014

"I have come to a still, but not a deep center,
A point outside the glittering current;
My eyes stare at the bottom of a river,
At the irregular stones, iridescent sandgrains,

My mind moves in more than one place,
In a country half-land, half-water.
I am renewed by death, thought of my death,
The dry scent of a dying garden in September,
The wind fanning the ash of a low fire.
What I love is near at hand,
Always, in earth and air."

Theodore Roethke (1908-1963)
The Far Field[74]

Subject: Diana's Detour 295
Tuesday, Sep 9, 2014

"Our fear of death is like our fear that summer will be short, but
when we have had our swing of pleasure, our fill of fruit,
and our swelter of heat, we say we have had our day."

—John Donne, 1620 (1572–1631)[75]

Subject: Diana's Detour 296
Wednesday, Sep 10, 2014

Windows open, eyes closed
Night sounds ringing
Bringing the stars in with them.

I can't believe that one source had lopped off the last two
stanzas of the following poem that I sent around a couple of
days ago.
Then again, shortened, perhaps it had more impact.
Here is the full poem.

September Midnight[76]
Sara Teasdale (1914)

Lyric night of the lingering Indian Summer,
Shadowy fields that are scentless but full of singing,
Never a bird, but the passionless chant of insects,
Ceaseless, insistent.
The grasshopper's horn, and far-off, high in the maples,
The wheel of a locust leisurely grinding the silence
Under a moon waning and worn, broken,
Tired with summer.
Let me remember you, voices of little insects,
Weeds in the moonlight, fields that are tangled with asters,
Let me remember, soon will the winter be on us,
Snow-hushed and heavy.
Over my soul murmur your mute benediction,
While I gaze, O fields that rest after harvest,
As those who part look long in the eyes they lean to,
Lest they forget them.

Subject: Diana's Detour 297
Thurs, Sep 11, 2014

Thirteen years after 9/11

I Saw You Walking[77]
Deborah Garrison

I saw you walking through Newark Penn Station
in your shoes of white ash. At the corner
of my nervous glance your dazed passage

first forced me away, tracing the crescent
berth you'd give a drunk, a lurcher, nuzzling
all comers with ill will and his stench, but
not this one, not today: one shirt arm's sheared
clean from the shoulder, the whole bare limb
wet with muscle and shining dimly pink,
the other full-sheathed in cotton, Brooks Bros.
type, the cuff yet buttoned at the wrist, a
parody of careful dress, preparedness—
so you had not rolled up your sleeves yet this
morning when your suit jacket (here are
the pants, dark gray, with subtle stripe, as worn
by men like you on ordinary days)
and briefcase (you've none, reverse commuter
come from the pit with nothing to carry
but your life) were torn from you, as your life
was not. Your face itself seemed to be walking,
leading your body north, though the age
of the face, blank and ashen, passing forth
and away from me, was unclear, the sandy
crown of hair powdered white like your feet, but
underneath not yet gray—forty-seven?
forty-eight? the age of someone's father—
and I trembled for your luck, for your broad,
dusted back, half shirted, walking away;
I should have dropped to my knees to thank God
you were alive, o my God, in whom I don't believe.

Subject: Diana's Detour 298
Fri, Sept. 12, 2014

Overwhelmed at home by mail and books
Overwhelmed at work by files and papers
Overwhelmed outside by leaves and weeds
Overwhelmed inside by promises and procrastination
Overwhelmed by the people I have not said appropriate thanks to
For their overwhelming hospitality and generosity
Overwhelmed by the fact that we moved back to DC from San Diego
One month before 9/11.
But I was glad we were here rather than there for the tragedy.
So I held a big 50th birthday party for myself two months later
To celebrate that we were still alive.
Overwhelmed to be alive, in fact, considering.

Subject: Re: Diana's Detour 299
Sat, Sept 13, 2014

"My husband is not wild about my behavior at these things," said a friend of mine, after walking out of a meeting about a massive apartment building being planned for our tiny metro parking lot.

She had written, "Leave it alone!" in magic marker (that they provided) on several of the many, often inaccurate, drawings the developers were ostensibly sharing for "community input,"

Input which, as one vocal African American attendee stated, is "oxymoronic."

"Well, at least no one is against the idea in principle anymore" stated one of the EYA facilitators sitting at a "discussion" session.
I raised my hand and emphatically stated, "I am!"

Developers come into our community and want to make it Rosslyn.

How many times has this area been protected by its residents' power of saying "no."

"No" to the Armenian Canadian brothers who wanted to develop Silver Spring into a massive amusement park.

"Something just has to be done about Silver Spring," tut-tutted one Potomac matron, as if it were a shared blight to be solved by someone living in a more exclusive area.

But by the power of "no," Silver Spring waited for Borders and Whole Foods to anchor their shopping district, and got NOAA and Discovery Communications to place their headquarters there. And the American Film Institute.

And no to changing my street, Piney Branch, into four lanes going into DC in the morning, and four lanes going out in the evening rush hour.

No to making Philadelphia aka Route 410 aka East-West Highway into the four lanes it is everywhere else.

You have to slow down for Takoma.
Human beings live here.
Our kids walk to school along those streets.
This is a living community.

But always under attack by people with money-making ideas to pitch.
That, incidentally, would gut the area of what makes it a desirable place to live.

Then again, I am shocked to be called a "have" by the "have not" young couples testifying on behalf of the apartment complex to be built.
"You people with your single family homes and your deep lots, you don't want to share."

With so much building going on around the metro, why do seven acres with 200 trees and a parking lot that was set aside for "transit-oriented development" have to be built upon?

It saddens me to see many of my fellow residents resigned to agreeing that every area needs to be filled.
But it gladdens me that others are demanding that zoning and height restrictions and encoded accessibility requirements be adhered to, so perhaps this debacle can be postponed into infinity.
It's already been delayed by a decade.
Yes!

Subject: Diana's Detour 300
Sunday, Sept 14, 2014

A glorious autumn Sunday at Longwood Gardens near Philadelphia
The Du Pont family's thousand acre estate.
Ballrooms of exotic potted plants
Italianate fountain gardens,
with a 2pm water display that can only be compared to fireworks;
formal flower garden walks
tumbling with sages, dahlias, coleus, canna
And then
A new outdoors.

"More than three miles of mown paths and boardwalk wind through and around an 86-acre field of grasses and wildflowers. Fresh and green when completed in June, the Meadow Garden is now tall and daubed with patches of color — the butter yellow of sunflowers, the muddy violet of the joe-pye weed, the intense purple of the ironweed. The meadow is full of bees and butterflies, and goldfinches seem to dance above it."

"There is something about the meadow that reaches deep; it is vital and still, nostalgic and bleak — like the memories of childhood and of dreams. It has reduced some visitors to tears, ... "It's the influence of the plants, the wind, the sky, the sun, the moon. There's something underlying there, in the pysche." Perhaps that is why visitors have been arriving in unanticipated numbers to savor it."

And my reality check was this:

"But for all its unfettered dynamism, the meadow on its own would be lost to neglect: Tree and shrub seedlings would grow and change its character, and invasive weeds and vines would smother much of the flora. In its first three years, the unwanted weeds must be removed diligently. (This is why the promise of a low-maintenance meadow as a landscape feature is so elusive.)

The woodies and weeds will be held back through early spring mowing and burning, timed to protect the meadow's cycles of insect and bird life."

So much work.
So much beauty.
I bow my head.

http://www.washingtonpost.com/lifestyle/style/at-longwood-gardens-a-new-meadow-for-the-ages/2014/09/07/b5c34a72-271c-11e4-958c-268a320a60ce_story.html

Subject: Diana's Detour 301
Mon, Sep 15, 2014

A picnic for 200 in a week.
It hasn't rained on that day in 7 years.
I hope my luck holds out.

Had to wear a sweater today.
Have to rip out crabgrass and put in seed.
It really is September.

Bought blue tulips at Longwood.
And a dainty feathery perennial called Gaura.
My faith in the future is boundless.

Subject: Diana's Detour 302
Tues, Sept 16, 2014

A nice thought for everyone who does have grandchildren.
If my children wait until their late thirties to have children,
as I did, then I'll be in my 70s when they have their babies.
And will I be around that long?....

Grandchildren[78]
by Olivia Stiffler

They disappear with friends
near age 11. We lose them
to baseball and tennis, garage
bands, slumber parties, stages
where they rehearse for the future,
ripen in a tangle of love knots.
With our artificial knees and hips
we move into the back seats
of their lives, obscure as dust
behind our wrinkles, and sigh
as we add the loss of them
to our growing list of the missing.

Sometimes they come back,
carting memories of sugar cookies
and sandy beaches, memories of how
we sided with them in their wars
with parents, sided with them

even as they slid out of our laps
into the arms of others.

Sometimes they come back
and hold onto our hands
as if they were the thin strings
of helium balloons
about to drift off.

Subject: Diana's Detour 303
Wed, Sept 17, 2014

The doctor's office called to say that I could still have my scan on Friday
but my doctor had to reschedule
So I won't get the results for another week or 10 days.

That's a normal wait for some people
However, I've been spoiled by getting results within an hour.

I don't mind waiting.
I just hope my doctor cancelled to do something fun and relaxing.
But I kind of doubt it.
She probably went off to a conference or workshop to learn more.
(Actually, she wound up having emergency surgery herself, but showed up at work within a few days)

I can't imagine the stress and depression that must go into being an oncologist.

My greatest respect goes to those in the medical profession.
I am in awe of the doctors and nurses I have had.
Not just their knowledge, but their caring.

I saw my oncologist every time I got chemotherapy.
I had the same nurse every time.

Our bodies are the lowest common denominator of our humanity.
I have been blessed with healthy genes
I have been blessed to live where clean water is a given
And refuse is removed, sanitized, not an issue.

The payment part of it is ridiculous
Had I not had excellent health insurance, I am afraid I would be bankrupt
Or at least my healing would have been less effective
If only for the stress attached to deductibles and percentages not covered.
But that is one issue so far beyond my ability to affect
That I cannot worry about it.

Have to worry about saying a few words at the rally for Ukraine Thursday afternoon in front of the White House.
And submitting an annual report.
And planning this weekend's picnic.

Sometimes I think it's worry that keeps me upright.

Subject: Diana's Detour 304, 305, 306, 307
Sun, Sep 21, 2014

Wiped out, literally, from the picnic for 200 today.
Shopped for days.
Drove up to Baltimore to pick up 80 lbs of sausage.
And two five-gallons tubs of vinegretas, a melange of peas
and carrots and dill, etc.
The woman who prepares this does it on the side at her
home.
She works in a nursing home full time.
Her house was immaculate.
I am so impressed.

Totally exploited my daughter and my nephew today at the
picnic.
Who worked for hours (at the bar and at the grill,
respectively).

"Where do you get your energy?" I asked my nephew.
"I'm forty years younger than you are," he dead-panned.

Getting scan results Monday afternoon.

Subject: Diana's Detour 308
Monday, Sept 22, 2014

My second scan came back clear!
I am home free.

Now, I will be getting a scan every three months until June
2016.

Then every six months until I hit the five-year mark.
And once a year until it's been ten years.
I may actually see a retirement!
Maybe even grandchildren...

So I think (as my daughter has suggested to me) it's time to end this "Detour."
Thank you so much for going on it with me.

The symptoms started last Labor Day.
I had surgery last October 9th, and then 5 months of systemic poisoning.

I was very scared at the beginning of my chemotherapy last November,
but it has helped me to write this
and to share my thoughts openly.

I have been profoundly touched by the outpouring of love and support from everyone.
Every prayer whispered and every candle lit
and every healing power invoked has helped so much.

I have also found that poetry says a lot.

Somehow, it felt only natural, after describing the experience of chemotherapy, to segue into poetry to try to make sense of it all. I had, after all, been put on a path that could lead to only one of two places ~ death or borrowed time. Either outcome stops one dead in one's tracks. I grasped at straws, and poetry answered.

How? I wish I could say. Even as an English major in college, I did not particularly care for poetry (my apologies to all my professors!). Give me a Thomas Hardy novel any day, any novel, just not a volume of poetry.

But poetry takes unexpected leaps and makes recognizable associations. It packages human experience into nugget form, and those nuggets are exquisite when you come across them. Sometimes they are just the turn of a phrase; other times, a complete vignette. But each contains its own "aha!" moment.

And nature just plain intruded itself into everything!
It really did.
Those birds. That snow. Those canyons. The wind.
In the enforced solitude of disease, nature moved from background to foreground.
It forced me to pause, to listen, to reflect.
And poetry captured what I heard at that moment.

One is not alone. Grief, love, fear, and wonder are shared by us all.
Poetry leaves us feeling vulnerably human, yet validated in our humanity.
Across centuries. Across continents. Across races. Across cultures.

I understand a poem is considered good if it can survive translation.
That seems counter-intuitive, since poetry depends so much upon the interplay of the sounds of words in one language. There must be something else at work there. Something was captured that was universal; something perhaps magical, something that could be shared.

* * *

Blasphemy[79]
For Sam Hamill
By Martin Espada (b. 1957)

Let the blasphemy be spoken: poetry can save us,
not the way a fisherman pulls the drowning swimmer
into his boat, not the way Jesus, between screams,
promised life everlasting to the thief crucified beside him
on the hill, but salvation nevertheless.

Somewhere a convict sobs into a book of poems
from the prison library, and I know why
his hands are careful not to break the brittle pages.

* * *

Autumn is my favorite season.
I am glad I am around for another one.
So I leave you with some poems I came upon recently.
I just realized there is a cricket in every one...

The Lake Isle of Innisfree[80]
by William Butler Yeats

I will arise and go now, and go to Innisfree,
And a small cabin build there, of clay and wattles made:
Nine bean-rows will I have there, a hive for the honeybee,
And live alone in the bee-loud glade.
And I shall have some peace there, for peace comes dropping
*   slow,*
Dropping from the veils of the morning to where the cricket
*   sings;*
There midnight's all a glimmer, and noon a purple glow,
And evening full of the linnet's wings.
I will arise and go now, for always night and day

I hear lake water lapping with low sounds by the shore;
While I stand on the roadway, or on the pavements grey,
I hear it in the deep heart's core.

The Sorrel Filly[81]
by Wendell Berry

The songs of small birds fade away
into the bushes after sundown,
the air dry, sweet with goldenrod.
Beside the path, suddenly, bright asters
flare in the dusk. The aged voices
of a few crickets thread the silence.
It is a quiet I love, though my life
too often drives me through it deaf.
Busy with costs and losses, I waste
the time I have to be here—a time
blessed beyond my deserts, as I know,
if only I would keep aware. The leaves
rest in the air, perfectly still.
I would like them to rest in my mind
as still, as simply spaced. As I approach,
the sorrel filly looks up from her grazing,
poised there, light on the slope
as a young apple tree. A week ago
I took her away to sell, and failed
to get my price, and brought her home
again. Now in the quiet I stand
and look at her a long time, glad
to have recovered what is lost
in the exchange of something for money.

J. Keats
Ode to Autumn[82]

SEASON of mists and mellow fruitfulness,
Close bosom-friend of the maturing sun;
Conspiring with him how to load and bless
With fruit the vines that round the thatch-eaves run;
To bend with apples the moss'd cottage-trees,
And fill all fruit with ripeness to the core;
To swell the gourd, and plump the hazel shells
With a sweet kernel; to set budding more,
And still more, later flowers for the bees,
Until they think warm days will never cease;
For Summer has o'erbrimm'd their clammy cells.

Who hath not seen thee oft amid thy store?
Sometimes whoever seeks abroad may find
Thee sitting careless on a granary floor,
Thy hair soft-lifted by the winnowing wind;
Or on a half-reap'd furrow sound asleep,
Drowsed with the fume of poppies, while thy hook
Spares the next swath and all its twinèd flowers:
And sometimes like a gleaner thou dost keep
Steady thy laden head across a brook;
Or by a cyder-press, with patient look,
Thou watchest the last oozings, hours by hours.

Where are the songs of Spring? Ay, where are they?
Think not of them, thou hast thy music too, —
While barrèd clouds bloom the soft-dying day
And touch the stubble-plains with rosy hue;
Then in a wailful choir the small gnats mourn
Among the river-sallows, borne aloft
Or sinking as the light wind lives or dies;

And full-grown lambs loud bleat from hilly bourn;
Hedge-crickets sing; and now with treble soft
The redbreast whistles from a garden-croft;
And gathering swallows twitter in the skies.

Post Script

It has now been two years since I finished chemotherapy and, I must say, I feel as if the cancer had never happened. How is it that I was so lucky?

And others were not. My friend who was diagnosed with lung cancer in March succumbed in December. In the harsh irony that is life, she had never touched a cigarette, but lung cancer in non-smokers is particularly deadly.

A beautiful artistic young mother in Takoma Park who had rented my home when we were in California died after battling many forms of cancer over the past few years. I wish I had taken the trouble to get to know her better.

A year ago, my lovely and fit sister-in-law got the same bleeding that I had had, and was diagnosed with a different cancer that had already metastasized. She had to undergo chemotherapy, then a full hysterectomy, then more chemotherapy. But her scans did not come back clear. She has a loving husband and three wonderful adult children who are now fully "launched" after college with promising careers. She is a study in gratitude, opting for a baseball cap rather than a wig, not wanting to discuss her prospects, preferring to live in the present, what's left of it.

I can now say that I feel lucky to have had the experience of cancer, and embarrassingly lucky to have gotten out alive, with no lasting side effects. I remember my caroling neighbor, who later died, told me he had to stop reading my posts because they were too perky, and he was jealous that I was able to eat food.

My experience tells me that when someone is diagnosed with cancer, they should know that it's not necessarily a death sentence. Sometimes, I think the doctors feel obliged to give you the worst-case scenario.

And no matter how much you trust your doctor, do not be afraid or embarrassed about getting a second, third, and fourth opinion. A doctor worth their salt will not feel threatened or offended. In fact, in my case, the doctors served on the same tumor review panel and debated the various treatment options for me because they even differed among themselves.

Plus, it helps to read up on your disease. It was my own reading that led me to turn down the radiation. I know my doctor meant well, and to her that meant doing absolutely everything so that her conscience could be clear that no stone had been left unturned. But if that additional treatment does not extend your life, why do it?

And it's the quality of that extended life that counts. One should always ask, what does this treatment buy me? What damage can it do to me? And what happens if I don't take it? Sometimes, the difference is not so great.

One must also realize that cancer is fickle, and each person's body reacts differently. The ifosfamide/paclitaxel chemotherapy combination that worked for me did not work for other patients with the exact same diagnosis. Go figure.

And everyone should respect that the journey someone takes with cancer is a very private one. You are facing your own mortality, and that is pretty scary.

Some people will want to share the details of their diagnosis and treatment. Others will want people to ignore the wig they're obviously wearing and not ask about it. Respect their choice, and don't push your own experience or that of others onto them.

Which perhaps begs the question, why this book? Only because someone suggested it might be helpful to others, as I seem to have had a positive experience with this very frightening thing called cancer. To show that it is possible. Otherwise, the contents certainly would have stayed just old emails to my friends.

Although I clung to the goal of working full time as a way to deal with my own disease, others find it healthier to cease devoting themselves to making a living and instead to abundantly living out the time that they have left. After all, no one on their deathbed ever said, "I wish I'd spent more time at my job."

However you decide to deal with your diagnosis, love life. Experience as much of its beauty as possible, whether it be walks in the neighborhood or making a pilgrimage to hike the 500 mile Camino de Santiago in Northern Spain. Feel your body in this world. Let it sense its wonders. We don't have all that much time here. And if it turns out that heaven actually was here on earth, what a pity not to have noticed and fully enjoyed it.

One suggestion I would make, however, is that this is the time to tell that person with cancer whom you know and love that you want them to live. It can make all the difference.

And my young friend with the non-Hodgkin lymphoma? She's currently pregnant with their first child.

Works Cited / Permissions

[1] "Hymn to God, My God, in My Sickness" by John Donne, 1572 – 1631. This poem is in the public domain.

[ii] "On the Beach at Night Alone" by Walt Whitman, 1819-1892. This poem is in the public domain.

[3] "Farewell, a long farewell to all my greatness!" by William Shakespeare, 1564-1616. From "Henry The Eighth," Act 3, scene 2. This play is in the public domain.

[4] "Because I Could Not Stop for Death." *THE POEMS OF EMILY DICKINSON: VARIORUM EDITION*, edited by Ralph W. Franklin, Cambridge, Mass.: The Belknap Press of Harvard University Press, copyright @ 1998 by the President and Fellows of Harvard College. Copyright @ 1951, 1955 by the President and Fellows of Harvard College. Copyright @ renewed 1979, 1983 by the President and Fellows of Harvard College. Copyright @ 1914, 1918, 1919, 1924, 1929, 1930, 1932, 1935, 1937, 1942 by Martha Dickinson Bianchi. Copyright @ 1952, 1957, 1958, 1963, 1965 by Mary L. Hampson.

[5] "The Granite Pail" from *The Granite Pail* by Lorine Niedecker, Gnomon Press; Revised edition (October 1, 1996), Permission given by Bob Arnold, Literary Executor for the Estate of Lorine Niedecker.

[6] "As if on a winter's night you sit feasting," by St. Bede, author of *Ecclesiastical History of the English People*, 672-735. This work is in the public domain.

[7] "When Lilacs Last in the Dooryard Bloom'd" by Walt Whitman, 1819-1892. This poem is in the public domain.

[8] "I Live My Life In Ever Widening Rings" from *The Book Of Hours*, by Rainer Maria Rilke, Translated from German by Paul Weinfield, © 2014. Permission granted by Paul Weinfield.

[9] "Our Ground Time Here Will Be Brief". Copyright © 1982 by Maxine Kumin, from *Selected Poems* 1960-1990 by Maxine Kumin. Used by permission of W.W. Norton & Company, Inc.

[10] "Snow-Flakes" by Henry Wadsworth Longfellow, 1807–1882. This poem is in the public domain.

[11] "January cold and desolate" by Christina Georgina Rossetti, 1830-1894. Rossetti's text from *Sing-Song – A Nursery Rhyme Book* published in 1893 is in the public domain.

[12] "March" from Small Rain by Barbara Crooker, Purple Flag Press, 2014. Permission granted by the author.

[13] "A Minor Poet" by Stephen Vincent Benét, 1898 – 1943. This poem is in the public domain.

[14] "I Have a Rendezvous with Life" by Countee Cullen, 1903-1946. This poem is in the public domain.

[15] "The thought manifests itself…" attributed to Buddha, c. 563 BCE/480 BCE – c. 483 BCE/400 BCE). These thoughts are in the public domain.

[16] "I wandered lonely as a cloud" by William Wordsworth, 1770-1850. This poem is in the public domain.

[17] "To Daffodils" by Robert Herrick, 1591-1674). This poem is in the public domain.

[18] "Prairie Spring" by Willa Cather, 1873-1947. This poem is in the public domain.

[19] "Easter" by Joyce Kilmer, 1886-1918. This poem is in the public domain.

[20] "Ode to a Hummingbird" in Fifty Odes, Poetry by Pablo Neruda, translated by George Schade, Host Publications, 2006. Permission granted by the publisher.

[21] "The Bluebell" by Anne Bronte, 1820-1849. This poem is in the public domain.

[22] "As long as this exists," Excerpt(s) from *THE DIARY OF A YOUNG GIRL: THE DEFINITIVE EDITION* by Anne Frank, edited by Otto H. Frank and Mirjam Pressler, translated by Susan Massotty, translation copyright © 1995 by Doubleday, a division of Random House LLC. Used by permission of Doubleday, an imprint of the Knopf Doubleday Publishing Group, a division of Penguin Random House LLC. All rights reserved.

[23] "My Summer in a Garden" by Charles Dudley Warner, 1829-1900. This poem is in the public domain.

[24] "When I have time to take a walk" by Chade-Meng Tan (Chinese: 陳一鳴), known informally as Meng, is a former software engineer and motivator known as the Jolly Good Fellow at the Google campus. Used by permission of the author.

[25] From the song, "God Bless the Grass." Words and music by Malvina Reynolds, Copyright 1964 Schroder Music Co (ASCAP). Renewed 1992. Used by permission. All rights reserved.

[26] "To the Virgins to Make Much of Time" by Robert Herrick, 1591-1674). This poem is in the public domain.

[27] "To His Coy Mistress" by Andrew Marvell, 1621-1678. This poem is in the public domain.

[28] "Ten Thousand Flowers in Spring" by Wu-Men [4.1] from *THE ENLIGHTENED HEART: AN ANTHOLOGY OF SACRED POERTY,*

CPSIA information can be obtained
at www.ICGtesting.com
Printed in the USA
BVOW03s1322090817
491621BV00001B/23/P

9 781632 133366